Just Plane Smart

Ed Sobey

**LEARNING
TRIANGLE
PRESS**

*Connecting
kids, parents, and teachers
through learning*

An imprint of McGraw-Hill

New York San Francisco Washington, D.C. Auckland Bogotá Caracas
Lisbon London Madrid Mexico City Milan Montreal New Delhi
San Juan Singapore Sydney Tokyo Toronto

A Division of The McGraw-Hill Companies

Other books by Ed Sobey:
Wrapper Rockets and Trombone Straws: Science at Every Meal
Car Smarts: Activities for Activities for Kids on the Open Road

Published by Learning Triangle Press, an imprint of McGraw-Hill.

pbk   2 3 4 5 6 7 8 9 KGP/KGP 9 0 3 2 1 0 9 8

ISBN 0-07-059598-4 (pbk.)

Library of Congress Cataloging-in-Publication Data

Sobey, Edwin J.C.,
    Just Plane Smart! / Ed Sobey.
      p.   cm.
    Summary: Presents activities, riddles, trivia, puzzles and more
  related to airplane travel.
    ISBN 0-07-059598-4 (pbk.)
    1. Games for travelers--Juvenile literature.   2. Aeronautics-
  -Juvenile literature.   3. Air Travel--Juvenile literature.
  [1. Aeronautics.   2. Air Travel.   3. Games for travelers.
  4. Games.] I. Title.
  GV1206.S673   1998
JQ 794--dc21
                            97-44425
                             CIP
                             AC

McGraw-Hill books are available at special quantity discounts to use as premiums and sales promotions. For more information, please write to the Director of Special Sales, McGraw-Hill,
11 West 19th Street, New York, NY 10011. Or contact your local bookstore.

Acquisitions editor: Judith Terrill-Breuer

Acknowledgments

Thank you. . . to John Manuszak and the enthusiastic staff of the Federal Aviation Administration at the Fresno Yosemite International (FYI) airport for showing
me their traffic control center; to SkyWest Station Manager Julie Brunn; to Ramp Supervisors Mark Cruise and Robert Earhart, who gave me a behind-the-scenes tour
of their operation at FYI; to Lala Guana at the Kitty Hawk restaurant, who took me into the kitchen to see how in-flight meals are prepared and delivered; to United
Airlines Maintenance Instructor James Chow for answering a host of questions and sharing with me his love of airplanes; and to Judith Terrill-Breuer, Editor-in-Chief
at McGraw-Hill, and her staff.

Contents

Dedication

to Margot,

who was born with the
desire to travel
and has seen the world

THINK ABOUT IT:

- You and a half million pounds of aluminum, baggage, and other people can fly through the air supported only by air flowing over the wings.
- You can circle the world in hours, but in your grandparents' time it would have taken weeks or months.
- Pioneers took six months to travel the Oregon Trail. You can fly the same route in a morning.
- And you can travel in nearly any weather, any day of the year, and in greater safety than ever before in human history.

Ever wonder how? People and technology, that's how, and science. Try this puzzle. If you can't finish it, that's ok. You'll be able to after you look at this book.

See if you can find the names of these famous people associated with aviation:

Bell
Bleriot
Boeing
Curtiss
Earhart
Jannus
Lindbergh
Montgolfier
Orville
Wilbur
Yeager

```
T  Y  B  E  L  L  I  C  T  G  D
O  B  O  E  I  N  G  U  Z  L  B
W  J  A  N  N  U  S  R  E  M  Y
Q  E  U  P  D  K  J  T  P  A  E
I  W  I  L  B  U  R  I  P  A  A
X  S  E  M  E  X  C  S  E  C  G
E  V  X  I  R  L  U  S  L  R  E
M  O  N  T  G  O  L  F  I  E  R
I  E  A  R  H  A  R  T  N  A  S
S  T  O  R  V  I  L  L  E  D  D
M  P  B  L  E  R  I  O  T  Y  A
```

  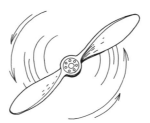  

Chapter 1

ATL, ORD, AND DFW: AIRPORTS

Airports are transportation centers where planes, trains, cars, conveyor belts, and electric carts help get you where you want to go.

Airports are like cities, too. They have their own police and fire departments, restaurants, stores, and parking garages. They have repair shops for planes and equipment. Hundreds or thousands of people work here, and something is always happening.

Checking Your Luggage?

You can check your luggage curbside, check it inside with the ticket agent, or carry it on board.

"Oh, are we over our limit?"

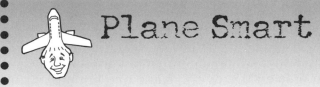

Plane Smart

➤ **How Much Luggage Can a Plane Carry?**

Lots. A 747 can carry 3,400 pieces of luggage. That's about seven per passenger, but don't try to check more than two per person unless you are willing to pay extra. The additional space is used to fly cargo.

If you check it, will your luggage arrive at the same airport and at the same time you do? Once the agent puts a routing tag on your bags, she loads them onto a conveyor system or a cart to start them on a journey of their own. Imagine what your luggage would say if it could talk:

"We were at the airport and my owner just dropped me off at the counter, when the other human put me on this neat amusement ride, called a conveyor. There were lots of twists and turns and tunnels and stuff. The ride stopped at the luggage handling area, where baggage handlers read a tag on my handle so they knew which plane I was traveling on. I didn't want to get on the wrong plane and end up in some lost luggage closet. The handler threw me onto a cart, and I don't mind telling you it's a good thing I'm tough. See this scar I got? Anyway, he drove me and a bunch of strange luggage to the plane, where he tossed me up into the plane. I mean, this was a rough trip, and it was just starting."

When your bag comes off the airplane at the next stop, a ramp agent reads the tag again and directs it to your connecting flight or to the baggage claim area. If you switch airlines, a "baggage runner" picks up your bag, reads the tag telling which airline you are traveling on next, and delivers the bag to that airline. Then an agent with that airline reads the tag and sends your bag to the correct airplane.

In larger airports, agents use a bar code system that eliminates some of the work of reading tags and moving bags. Look to see if your luggage tag has a bar code, like the ones used on the products you buy at a grocery store. As the bags travel along conveyor belts, a laser beam flashes across the luggage, and the reflected light from the bar code tells a computer where to send your bag.

Don't worry.
Your bags will arrive okay.

Crazy Codes

Check out the airport codes on your luggage tag and in the airline schedule. Chicago's O'Hare Airport has a code of "ORD." How did someone come up with "ORD" for O'Hare? The airport, before it was named O'Hare, was built beside an orchard. So someone came up with ORD as a code for the orchard airport.

See if you can figure out which cities correspond with which airport codes.

AIRPORT CODES

Airport Code		City
1. DEN	____	Memphis, Tennessee
2. JAX	____	St. Louis, Missouri
3. FAI	____	Anchorage, Alaska
4. PDX	____	Oakland, California
5. TPA	____	Belize City, Belize
6. ATL	____	Portland, Oregon
7. IST	____	Salt Lake City
8. RDU	____	Tokyo, Japan
9. HNL	____	Chicago, Illinois
10. LIM	____	San Francisco, California
11. TGU	____	Dallas-Ft. Worth, Texas
12. YTO	____	Tegucigalpa Honduras
13. HND	____	Seattle, Washington
14. SEA	____	Edmonton, Alberta, Canada
15. OAK	____	Tampa, Florida
16. TYO	____	Honolulu, Hawaii
17. SLC	____	Atlanta, Georgia
18. BWI	____	Raleigh-Durham, North Carolina
19. SFO	____	Denver, Colorado
20. STL	____	Baltimore, Maryland
21. MEM	____	Jacksonville, Florida
22. ORD	____	Fairbanks, Alaska
23. BZE	____	Istanbul, Turkey
24. ANC	____	Lima, Peru
25. DFW	____	Toronto, Ontario
26. GEG	____	Spokane, Washington
27. SDA	____	Tokyo, Haneda, Japan
28. YEA	____	Baghdad, Iraq

See answers on page 87.

How Many Airports Are There?

There are approximately 1,000 airports in the United States big enough to accommodate large airplanes. However, if we count small airports as well as big ones, there are 11,000 airports in this country.

The Busiest Airports

Can you can guess the ten busiest airports in the world?

Here are the busiest airports and the number of passengers who used them.

THE WORLD'S BUSIEST AIRPORTS FOR 1995

Ranking	Airport	Millions of Passengers
1	Chicago O'Hare	67
2	Atlanta	58
3	London Heathrow	54
4	Dallas-Fort Worth	54
5	Los Angles	54
6	Tokyo Haneda	46
7	Frankfurt	38
8	San Francisco	36
9	Miami International	33
10	Denver	31

What's in a Name?

Airports in many cities are named for the city, but some are named for people or things.

Can you match the airport names with their locations?

1. O'Hare — __ San Diego
2. Dulles — __ Dallas
3. Logan — __ Atlanta
4. Sky Harbor — __ St. Louis
5. Midway — __ Wichita, Kansas
6. Hartsfield — __ Washington, D.C.
7. Kennedy — __ Las Vegas
8. Lindbergh — __ Cleveland
9. La Guardia — __ Orange County, California
10. Will Rogers — __ Phoenix
11. John Wayne — __ Oklahoma City
12. McCarran — __ Boston
13. National — __ Columbus
14. Hopkins — __ Portland
15. Mid-continent — __ Chicago
16. Rickenbacker — __ New York

See answers on page 87.

Feeling Secure?

On the way to your departure gate, you pass through a security check. There you put all the objects you are carrying onto a conveyor belt so the operator can look at them. The viewing machine makes x-rays, which pass through most materials but are stopped by metals and some other materials. By watching a television screen, the operator can see if there are any metal objects inside your bags.

Then you walk through a magnetic detector that senses if you are carrying metal. It's annoying if your belt buckle or coins in your pocket set off the alarm, but it's nice to know that no one can sneak a gun onto the plane.

METAL DETECTORS The magnetic detector works like the metal detector that senses the presence of your car to change traffic lights. These devices use electricity to make a magnetic field. If metal objects, like coins in your pocket or cars at an intersection, move into the magnetic field, they disrupt the field and set off the alarm or change the light. If you can't find the objects that set off the alarm, security guards search for them with a small hand magnetic detector called a wand.

Control Tower

The control tower, rising above the other buildings and covered with antenna, is the command center of the airport. From here, air traffic controllers direct planes on the ground and in the air.

Air traffic controllers are the airplane traffic police. As commercial airplanes fly across the country, air traffic controllers track their progress and make sure that they don't get too close to other airplanes.

When a plane approaches an airport, air traffic controllers tell the pilot which runway to use. Different sets of controllers give instructions to planes in different parts of the sky. When a plane crosses from one part to another, the controllers guiding the plane "pass off" the plane to the next group of controllers.

Air traffic controllers direct pilots on the ground and in the air.

Air Traffic Controllers

There are about 14,000 controllers at hundreds of stations across the United States. Many stations welcome visitors who call ahead. If you want to visit, look up the phone number in the government section of the phone book.

Ground controllers give directions to pilots to avoid collisions while taxiing on the ground. Pilots radio the ground controllers when they are ready to push back from the gate, and a controller, who has better visibility from the control tower, tells them when it's safe to go.

THE FIRST CONTROLLER The first equipment used to control airplanes in the United States included two flags and a wheelbarrow. In 1929, Archie League started hauling two flags, his lunch, and a thermos of coffee in a wheelbarrow onto the airfield in St. Louis. He signaled planes with a checkered flag to indicate it was safe to land or take off. The red flag meant stop.

LIGHTNING RODS Lightning rods are placed on the roofs of barns and some other buildings to attract lightning. The rods keep lightning from damaging the building because they are connected to wires leading to the ground, so the lightning's electrical energy travels along the wire and into the ground.

STRUCK BY LIGHTNING On average, lightning hits one hundred commercial airplanes each year.

But that's okay because the lightning seldom causes any damage, except to everyone's nerves. The electric charge doesn't penetrate the metal walls of the airplane due to its high frequency. You're sitting safely inside the plane while the electrical charges are contained on the outside. The same holds true for cars—a good place to take refuge during a lightning storm.

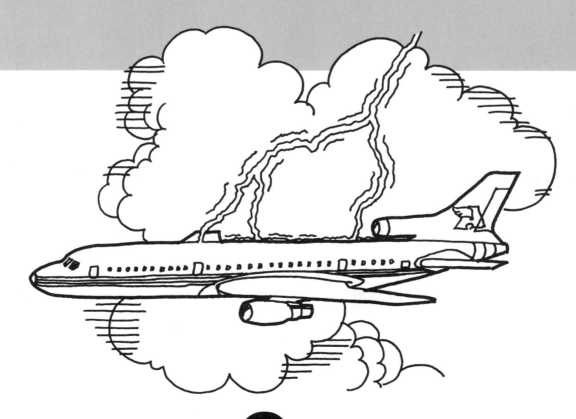

Check Out the Planes

Can you identify the different types of airplanes at your airport? Looking at the number of engines and their location will help you compare actual planes to the diagram.

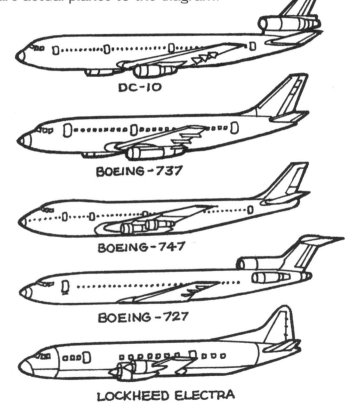

DC-10

BOEING-737

BOEING-747

BOEING-727

LOCKHEED ELECTRA

The more common airplanes you might see at an airport

BOEING The world's largest manufacturer of commercial aircraft is the Boeing Company located in Seattle, Washington. They build about 400 airliners each year.

PLANE LANGUAGE

The **fuselage** is the body of the plane. The **tail** sticks up at the end of the plane (where else?) and supports a horizontally mounted **elevator**. The tail stabilizes the plane so it doesn't swing from side to side. **Engines** can be mounted on the wings, fuselage, or even on the tail. How many sets of landing gear and wheels can you see on each plane? The number varies, so that's one way to tell planes apart.

Along the leading edges of wings, you should be able to see either a black or silver edge. That's the all-important **de-icer**. Planes flying through freezing rain can accumulate ice on their wings, and the de-icer gets rid of it. Planes with the silver edge melt the ice with hot exhaust gases from the engines. The black edge is an inflatable boot. When ice starts to build up on the wing, the pilot inflates the boot, which swells up and cracks the ice so it falls off.

On the wing, you should be able to see small tabs of metal sticking up about an inch also. These are **vortex generators** that swirl the air and help hold it close to the wing. Keeping the moving air close to the wing gives greater lift.

Since lift is what holds the plane up, plane designers want to get lots of it.

Slats provide additional lift. They extend forward from the leading edge of the wing.

Along the trailing edge of the wings, you will see four or five wires sticking backwards. They may look like tiny lightning rods, but they aren't there to attract lightning. Instead, they help electrical charges flow from the airplane to the atmosphere. The charges build up when a plane flies through the air, especially in storms.

Also along the trailing edge of the wings there are a series of **flaps**. The pilots can extend the flaps to give the wing a larger surface and more lift for take-offs and landings. Since planes have to go slowly for take-offs and landings, and since lift is lower at slow speeds, the pilot compensates by making the wings larger for more lift.

On top of the wings are flaps, called **spoilers**, that the pilot raises during landings. They help slow the airplane by adding drag, or wind resistance.

Ailerons are flaps that help roll or **bank** the airplane so it can turn. When an airplane turns, it lowers the wing on the inside of the turn and raises the wing on the outside. This is called banking. When you are flying, you can look out the window to see the ailerons change position when the plane starts a turn.

Near the front of the airplane, probably on the left side, you may see one or two small tubes sticking out of the fuselage. These are **pitot tubes**. They measure how fast the airplane is flying. As air rushes past the tubes, air pressure in them drops. The faster the plane flies, the lower the pressure becomes. So by measuring the pressure in the tubes, instruments can calculate the air speed of the plane. Pilots can read the speed of the plane on the air speed indicator.

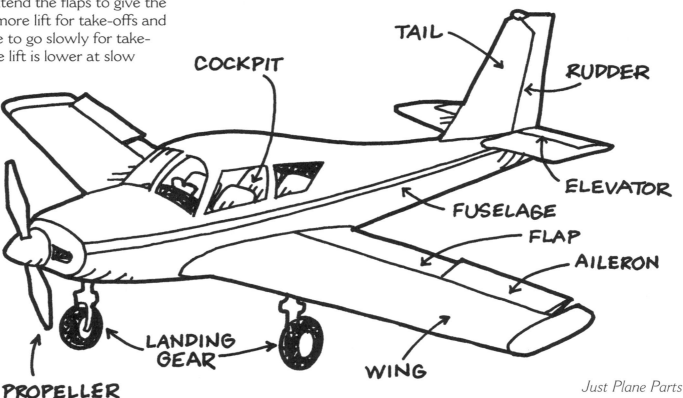

COCKPIT

TAIL

RUDDER

ELEVATOR

FUSELAGE

FLAP

AILERON

PROPELLER

LANDING GEAR

WING

Just Plane Parts

Try making a paper plane. If you don't have a piece of paper with you, look for a magazine left behind on one of the chairs and tear out a sheet. Once you have paper, fold it in half length-wise. Open up the fold so the paper is flat, and fold the corners at one end so they touch the mid-line of the paper.

Now fold the edges over again to the center line and crease them. Do this on both sides. Repeat the fold one more time on both sides. Fold the plane in half along the center line, but in the direction opposite to your first fold. Find a place where there aren't any other passengers and give it a gentle toss.

By making some cuts on the rear of your plane, you can see how ailerons and elevators work. Cut with scissors or tear along the third fold line on each side about a half inch in from the rear of the plane to make flaps. Now you are ready to adjust the flaps to make your plane fly up, down, or to the side.

Bend both flaps up slightly and give it a toss. If it doesn't fly at all, it has too much drag. To reduce the drag, try a smaller upward angle on the flaps. That is, don't bend them so far. After you have a successful flight, try bending the flaps downward and giving your plane a fling.

The flaps act like the elevator on a plane. If the pilot wants to fly higher, he raises the rear of the elevator. To go down, he lowers it.

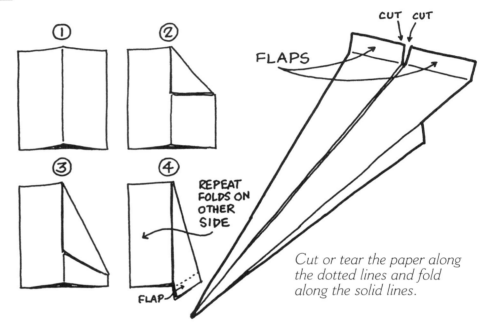

Cut or tear the paper along the dotted lines and fold along the solid lines.

Directions for making a model airplane.

Now, slightly bend one flap up and the other down. This is what ailerons do on an airplane. The pilot turns the aileron on one wing up, and the aileron on the other wing goes down. This rolls the plane into a turn, like you lean into a turn when riding a bike.

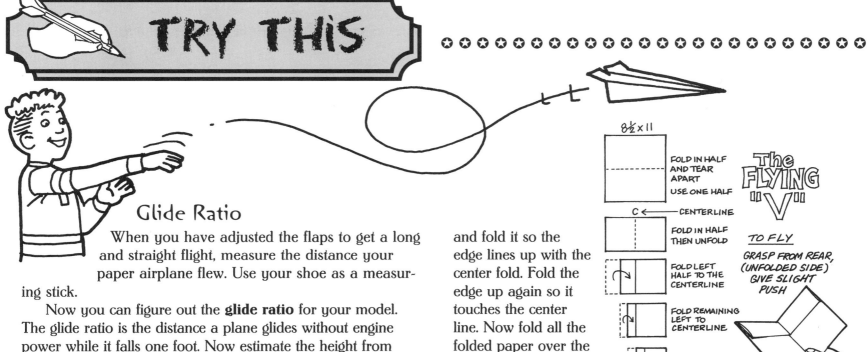

TRY THIS

Glide Ratio

When you have adjusted the flaps to get a long and straight flight, measure the distance your paper airplane flew. Use your shoe as a measuring stick.

Now you can figure out the **glide ratio** for your model. The glide ratio is the distance a plane glides without engine power while it falls one foot. Now estimate the height from which you launched it in shoe lengths.

Say you released your model at the height of six shoe lengths and it flew twenty-four shoe lengths before hitting the floor. Then the glide radio for that model is $24/6 = 4$. Engineers would say it has a glide ratio of "4 to 1."

Glide On and On: the Flying "V"

Fold a piece of paper in half lengthwise, crease it, and tear it along this line. Take one of the pieces of paper and fold it in half along its longer side. Open it up and use the center crease you just made as a guide for the next two folds. Take one end and fold it so the edge lines up with the center fold. Fold the edge up again so it touches the center line. Now fold all the folded paper over the original centerline. Use a coin to crease the folds firmly.

Now, fold the paper in half from side to side, but don't crease this fold. You want just a bend in the plane. Holding the plane by its tail, release it from as high as you can reach.

You can make minor adjustments by bending the back of the wings up (if it swoons downward) or down (if it climbs too steeply after you throw it).

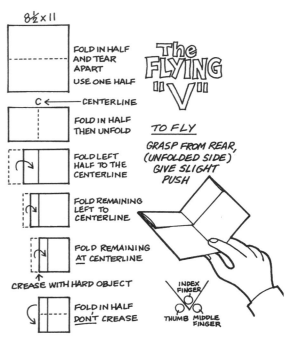

TRY THIS

Make Your Own Pitot Tube

You can see the pressure drop in a tube when air flows past it by blowing across the top of a straw in a soda. Hold the straw vertically in your drink and blow horizontally across the top of it. When you blow hard, soda rises in the straw. The strong wind reduced the pressure in the straw and, with less pressure above it, the soda moved up. If you can't blow cross the straw and watch the soda rise at the same time, get some one else to blow while you watch.

FAMOUS FLIGHT LOGS

➢ **First Flight**

The first person to fly was Pilatre de Rozier. In 1783 he flew in a hot air balloon designed and built by Etienne and Joseph Montgolfier of France.

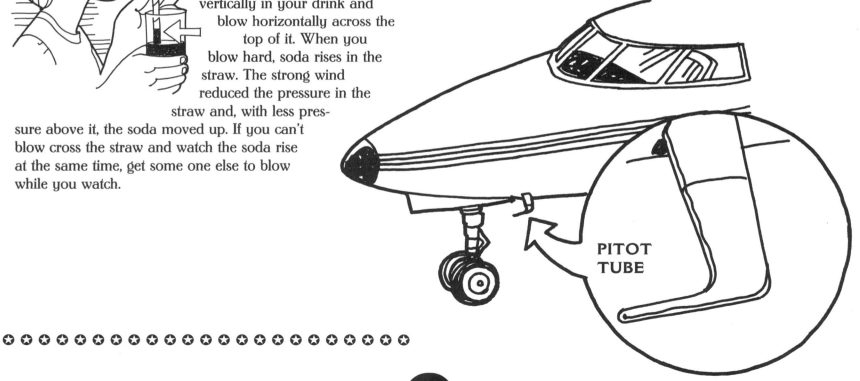

PITOT
TUBE

Jet or Piston Engines

Will you be flying in a plane with **jet** or **piston** engines? If your flight is more than 200 miles, your airplane will probably be a jet. Jets don't have propellers. But even if your plane has a propeller, it could be a jet-powered propeller airplane called a **turboprop**.

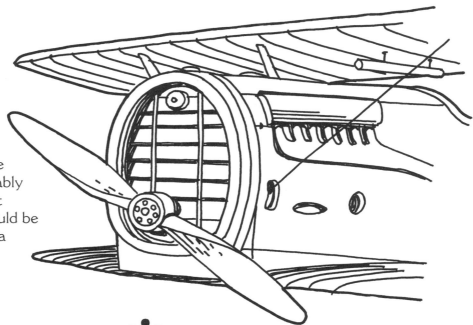

GEO-SMART

Which two states share borders with eight other states? Eight states share borders with six states and one state shares borders with seven states. Can you name the states that have the most neighbors?

Answer: Missouri and Tennessee have eight neighbors and Kansas has seven. The states with six neighbors are: Arkansas, Illinois, Iowa, Nebraska, Wyoming, Colorado, Idaho, and South Dakota.

WHY ARE AIRPLANE WINGS SHINY? The wings (and the rest of the airplane) are made mostly of aluminum, which reflects 80% of the light that strikes it. The light reflecting off the wings gives them the shiny appearance.

Why use aluminum for airplanes? It's strong, it's lightweight, and it doesn't require much maintenance.

Like piston engines, jets burn fuel, but the hot combustion gases don't push against pistons. Instead they expand (hot gases take up more space than do cold gases) and rush through a nozzle to provide thrust. Thrust pushes the plane forward, just as a balloon flies when you release air. The balloon and the jet engine release gas in one direction, which propels them in the opposite direction.

Look at a jet engine on the wing of a plane. The large opening on the forward side scoops air into the engine as the plane moves forward. The inside of the engine narrows to compress the air, and then fuel sprays into the air, and the air-fuel mixture ignites. The hot gases from the fire escape through the nozzle, which faces the rear of the plane. Hot gases moving in one direction push the plane in the opposite direction.

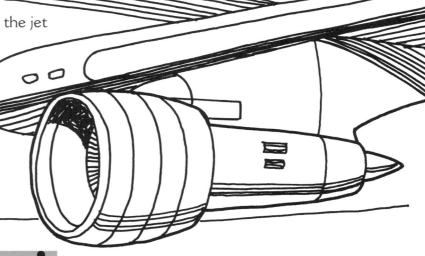

Plane Smart

➤ How Hot Is It?

Inside a jet engine, the burning fuel and air can reach temperatures as high as 3,600°F. That's hot enough to melt aluminum. Hey, isn't the engine made of aluminum? Is it going to melt?

Nope. Some of the air that enters the engine flows past the metal in the combustion chamber to cool it so it doesn't melt.

THE NOSE KNOWS. Notice that the noses of many planes are black. The nose is made of a material that allows radar waves to pass through it. Inside the nose is a radar system, and if the nose were made of aluminum like the rest of the plane, the radar signal couldn't get through. Radar, like light, reflects off aluminum.

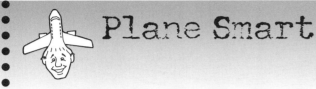

Plane Smart

➤ The First Commercial Jet Plane

The Boeing 707 was the first commercial jet airplane made in the United States. The prototype made its first flight near Seattle, Washington, in July, 1954.

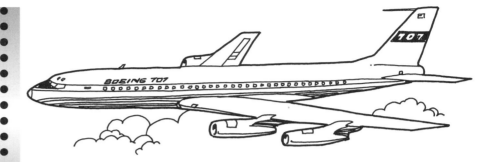

Airlines use jet engines because they make air travel less expensive. For two engines of equal weight, a jet engine produces a lot more power than a piston engine. Or, as engineers say, the "power-to-weight ratio" is much higher in a jet engine. The added power allows aircraft companies to design larger planes that fly faster than planes with piston engines.

Also they use less fuel and cost less to operate per mile of travel than piston engines.

FUEL IT UP Your car's engine probably burns gasoline or diesel fuel. Jet engines burn kerosene. Notice the smell of kerosene as you board your airplane. Remember that smell and compare it to the smell when you are filling up the gas tank in your car.

Better to Drive or Fly?

Does it cost more to fly than drive? It depends. Let's say you're going on a 500-mile trip. Traveling by car, you need to buy about twenty-five gallons of gasoline, assuming the car gets twenty miles per gallon.

On a 747, instead of miles per gallon, you measure consumption in *gallons per mile*. That's about six gallons per mile, or 33,000 gallons!

What's In A Name

Have you noticed the names companies give to their planes? Boeing uses numbers like 747 or 757 for names. Why does Boeing like "7_7"?

Boeing called their first plane "1." As they designed different planes, they started a three-digit name, like 200 or 300. When Boeing introduced their first jet airplane in the 1950s, they gave it the name of "707." Each major airline jet designed by Boeing since the 707 has been given a 7_7 name according to the order in which they are designed. Thus the 737 was designed after the 727. But don't go looking for a 717. There aren't any. For some reason Boeing skipped that number.

Other airline manufacturers have their own naming system. Lockheed's wide body jetliner is the L-1011. McDonnell-Douglas planes have names that start with MD, like the MD-80 and MD-90. Before Douglas merged with McDonnell, they numbered their models from the earliest, DC-1 to the most recent, DC-10.

TRY THIS

Are They Making a Profit?

If it costs an airline $13,000 to fly a plane from San Francisco to Los Angles how many seats do they have to sell to make money? Assume that the average ticket price is $175. If this plane holds 106 passengers, what is the percentage of seats the airline would need to sell to make a profit?

Answer: Profitable or not? If the airline sold more than 74 seats, it would earn a profit. With 106 seats on the plane, that means it needs to sell 70% of the available seats.

But wait a minute. In your car you could take a couple of friends; maybe you could take a total of four people. On the 747, you could invite your closest 400 friends and still have room for a few strangers. That changes things.

Now calculate the fuel used per passenger over the 500 mile trip. Your car will use twenty-five gallons, which is about six gallons per person. The 747 will use 3,000 gallons which is 7.5 gallons per person. That's pretty close. Take one person off the plane and one person out of the car, and the 747 wins the fuel economy test—7.5 gallons per person to 8.5 gallons per person in the car.

So how do driving and flying compare? To go to the supermarket to get a loaf of bread, there is no comparision. Driving is better. To cross a mountain pass in winter, cross an ocean, or travel thousands of miles, there is no comparison. Flying is better.

Gas up the plane

Gas up the car

The Great Car and Plane Race Puzzle

You start driving from city A toward city B along a straight freeway. The same instant you leave A, your friend departs B in an airplane and heads toward A. As soon as the plane is directly over the car, it turns around and goes back to B. When it gets to B, it turns around and heads back until it encounters the car again. The plane keeps flying back and forth until you arrive in B.

The car travels at 50 miles per hour, and the planes flies at 300 miles per hour. The two cities, A and B, are 500 miles apart. How many miles does the plane fly?

Hint: First figure out how long it will take the car to arrive and then figure out how many miles the plane will travel.

Answer: Puzzle. The plane will travel 3,000 miles. If it takes the car ten hours to go from A to B (500 miles at 50 miles per hour), and if the plane if flying the entire time the car is traveling (that is, it's flying ten hours at 300 miles per hour), the plane goes 3,000 miles.

✪ ✪ ✪ ✪ ✪ ✪ ✪ ✪ ✪

What Are All Those Trucks Doing?

Beefy-looking **push-back** tugs push large airliners back from the gate. Smaller tugs pull luggage trailers from planes to the luggage handling facilities. To load luggage inside the plane, there are conveyor belts on wheels or trucks called **belt loaders**. **Fuel trucks** drive to the planes to pump fuel into tanks.

Power to the plane! Tugs also pull carts that provide electrical power to planes. You might see the ground crew hook up wires from a cart to the plane. The cart has an electrical generator that burns fuel to make electricity. Planes need to keep the on-board computers going and the interior lights on. So either the plane uses its own generator or it gets power from a cart. The on-board generator is called an auxiliary power unit (APU), and the generator on the cart is called a GPU, a ground power unit.

Larger trucks bring in the food, utensils, and plates. A crew of people at the airport prepares the food before the flight. They drive their truck to the plane and, with a hydraulic lift, raise the back of the truck so it's the same height as the airplane's galley doors. The doors on most planes are on the **starboard** or right side, so they're not in the way of passengers entering and leaving on the **port**, or left side.

Plane Smart

> ## Where Is All the Fuel Stored?

In most planes, fuel tanks are located in the wings and fuselage. However, some airplanes also store fuel in the tail. A 747-400 can carry over 3,000 gallons of fuel in its tail, enough to fly the plane an additional 400 miles. To store all the fuel it needs, a 747 has twelve fuel tanks.

What Are Those Hoses Connected to the Plane?

On hot days you may see the ground crew hook up a big, yellow hose to a plane. This hose carries air-conditioned air into the plane. Small blue hoses connected to the underside of the plane supply fresh water for the lavatories. And, in case you were wondering, all the waste from the lavatories falls out into a large black tube (the "biffy tube") and is carted away and pumped into a sewer. So that's where it goes!

Runways

Boy, are they long. And we can be thankful, because long runways give pilots more time to accelerate for take-off and to slow down for landing. To take off, planes need to build up enough speed so the air traveling around the wings can suck the plane up off the ground. That takes a lot of speed.

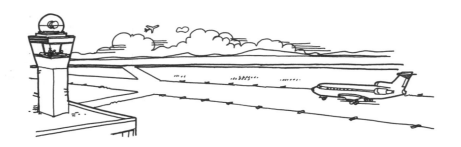

Plane Smart

> **Plane Language: Taxis and Aprons**
Aircraft park on the **loading apron**. They "taxi" on the **taxiway** to the **runway** where they can take off.

Most planes are moving at least 130 miles per hour, and some have to go 210 miles per hour, to take off. A 747 needs more than a mile of runway to reach take-off speed.

What Do You Call a Runway?

Runways are named for their compass direction. For example, if you are taking off on a runway heading due east, you're on runway 9. The 9 is short for 90 degrees, which is the compass heading for east. If you're on the same pavement, but heading due west, you'd call the runway 27 for 270 degrees. The runway orientated due north is 36 (since there are 360 degrees in a compass) and going in the opposite direction it is called 18. If the airport has two parallel runways, one is L for left and the other is R for right. So a runway heading east could be 9R or 9L.

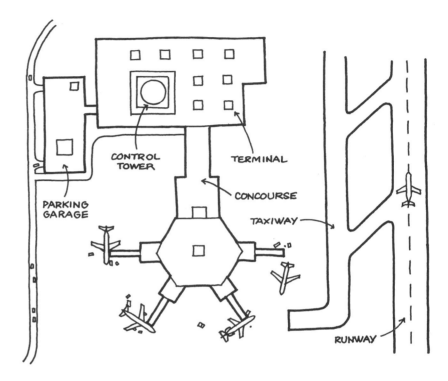

CONTROL TOWER

TERMINAL

CONCOURSE

PARKING GARAGE

TAXIWAY

RUNWAY

Plane Smart

➤ **Plane Language: Why Is It Called a "Runway?"**

Runways existed before airports. Runways were narrow ramps in night clubs where dancers could walk or dance from the stage into the audience. Before night clubs used the word runway, it was used for paths that deer follow through the woods.

THE LONGEST RUNWAY The world's longest runway is at Edwards Air Force Base in California. It is nearly seven and a half miles long.

That's A Lot of Land!

Miami International, the sixth busiest airport in the United States, has nearly 9,000 parking spaces. It has 102 passenger gates to serve 33 million passengers each year.

The Denver International Airport is the largest public works project ever completed in the United States. It covers 33,920 acres, or 53 square miles. That's bigger than a lot of cities. With 23,000 airport workers, it takes a big parking lot just to serve the people who work there.

As big as Denver's airport is, one in Saudi Arabia is much bigger. It covers 87 square miles.

FLYAWAY NEBRASKA

FAMOUS FLIGHT LOGS

➤ If At First You Don't Succeed. . .

That must have been the motto of aviator Louis Bleriot. Bleriot built and wrecked ten airplanes and endured dozens of crashes in his quest to fly across the English Channel. He succeeded in 1909 with his eleventh plane and was the first to fly across. It was good luck that allowed him to cross: A light rain cooled his engine. Without the rain, his engine would have overheated and sputtered to a stop long before he reached land. Not only was he the first to fly across the English Channel, but his was the first international flight.

2 TAKING OFF

Your captain pulls back from the gate and starts to taxi from the apron onto the runway. The flight attendant repeats the safety messages, your seat belt is snug and tight across your waist, and your tray table is stored in the upright position. You are ready for take-off.

Before the pilot can go anywhere, he has to contact ground control to request clearance to taxi. Controllers tell him which runway to use and where other planes are taxiing.

What Does the Wind Have to Do With It?

COCKPIT TOUR   Would you like to visit the cockpit? Before the flight took off and during the flight, regulations prohibit your visiting the flight deck. The best time to see it is when you land. Tell a flight attendant during the flight that you would like to visit the cockpit and see if he or she can arrange it.

Birds and planes head into the wind to take off. Both need air flowing over their wings to generate lift. If a bird can fly at 10 miles per hour, it can either wait for a 10-mile-per-hour breeze and face into it, or it can take off without a breeze by flapping itself into the air.

A 747 heading into a 40-mile-an-hour wind will take off at a ground speed of only 170 miles per hour. It will need less than 5,000 feet to reach that speed. However, if it were to take off with the wind going in the same direction, it would need a ground speed of 250 miles per hour and nearly 10,000 feet of runway, almost two miles. By taking off into the wind, an airplane uses lower ground speed and less runway. That's why federal regulations don't let airliners take off with more than a 12-mile-an-hour tailwind because the plane would have to travel too far along the runway trying to pick up enough air speed to take off.

Sitting at the end of the runway, with final take-off clearance, the captain and first officer push forward on the throttles, and the engines start to whine. As the captain releases the brakes, the plane moves forward. If you can see the wings from your seat, you'll see that the flaps are extended to give the plane the most lift. Once the plane is in the air, it moves fast enough for the wings to make enough lift without the flaps, so the pilot pulls them back into the wings. If you watch the wings, you'll see when the pilot does this.

As the plane accelerates, you feel pushed backwards against your seat. Actually, your seat is pushing *you* forward. The seat and the entire airplane are accelerating, and the seat is exerting a force on you.

When the plane is moving fast enough for the wings to provide enough lift to balance the weight of the plane, the captain pulls back on the yoke. Up you go.

YOUR FLIGHT LOG

The airplane crew fill out flight logs to record fuel consumption, the number of passengers, where and when they flew, and other details of a flight. You can keep a record of your plane trips by filling out your own flight log. The log will remind you of the details you would otherwise forget.

FLIGHT LOG

Date:_____

Flying from: _____   Flying to: _____

Stops: _____

Flying with _____   Alone _____

Airline(s): _____, _____

Types of Airplanes: _____, _____

Weather Conditions:_____

     Bumpy index: 1.___ (Smooth)

                      2.___ (I felt a bump or two)

                      3.___ (It was okay, really)

                      4.___ (I'm glad it's over)

                      5.___ (Yes, I did use a bag)

Cruising altitude: _____

Average air speed: _____ MPH

Length of flight: _____

Next to me was: _____

The movie was: _____

 Rating: ___ 👍 or ___ 👎

Meals and snacks: ___ 👍 or ___ 👎

What I saw out my window: _____

_____

The landing was: ___ (I could have slept through it)

                     ___ (Boring)

                     ___ (Average)

                     ___ (Interesting)

                     ___ (Exciting)

My luggage arrived: ___ (in the same airport as I did, at nearly

                         the same time)

                     ___ (in a different time zone)

                     ___ (we're still waiting)

Who was there to meet us: _____

_____

What we did at our destination: _____

_____

_____

Next destination: _____

_____

_____

GEO-SMART

If you took off from Santiago, Chile, and flew due north, which city would you fly over: Dallas, Denver, Boston, or San Francisco?

Boston is due north of Santiago, Chile.

Plane Smart

➤ They Never Took Off

The first airplane capable of vertical take-offs and landings was the Convair XFY-1, called the "Pogo." The plane sat vertically on its tail fins on the ground, and took off straight up, leveling off for horizontal flight after it was airborne. Although it flew, it never caught on.

Another idea that never took off was the Aerocar. Just the thing to beat the traffic rush, the Aerocar had wings that clipped onto the sides of the car for flight and were towed in a trailer when driving on a road. It took only five minutes to convert it from a car to a plane and could fly at 140 miles per hour. Sounds pretty good, doesn't it?

The yoke controls both the elevator, which is on the tail, and the ailerons, which are on the wings. By pulling back, the captain raises the elevator, which pushes the rear of the plane down and the front up.

The landing gear includes the tires, wheels, and the struts supporting the wheels. All this equipment sticking out below the airplane slows the plane. So, as soon as possible after take-off, the pilots pull up the landing gear.

TRY THIS

Listening to the Pilot

Check in the seat pocket for a headset or ask a flight attendant for a one. Many airlines let you listen to the radio communications between pilots and controllers.

Pilots identify their planes by giving their company and flight number. Listen for your flight number—it's on your ticket and boarding pass—as the pilot requests clearance for take-off. As soon as the controller tells the pilot it's safe to go, you'll feel the plane surge forward.

Keep listening after take-off. You'll hear controllers giving the pilots the course heading and altitude to fly. They also direct pilots to contact controllers in the next area, as the plane leaves the airport control area.

AIRLINE CALL SIGNS

As you listen to the radio, you might hear pilots using call signs *instead of their company name. Call signs are like nicknames used on the radio. Here are some of the more colorful ones.*

Cactus	American West	Mushroom	Western Kenya Aircharters
Wild Onion	Chicago Air	Pirate	Air South West (U.K.)
Top Hat	Northcoast Executive Airlines	Python	Performance Executive Airlines (U.K.)
Road Runners	Pacific International Airlines (Tucson)	Sage Brush	Pacific Coast Airlines (Newport Beach, Ca.)
Waterski	Trans World Express	Sinbad	Arab Air Cargo (Jordan)
Pee Jay	Private Jet Expeditions	Springbok	South African Airways
Critter	ValuJet Airlines	Stinger Bee	Eastwind Airlines, Inc. (Winston-Salem, N.C.)
Big Bird	Hungarian-Ukranian Airlines	Speedbird	British Airways

Birds, Bugs, and Airplanes

It seems that everyone has dreamed of flying. For many, copying birds seemed to make sense.

Things that flap to fly are called **ornithopters**—the word comes from the same word as ornithology (the study of birds) and ornithologists (people who study birds). Although many people have tried to make ornithopters fly, no one has succeeded. Yet.

One of the reasons is that birds don't just flap their wings up and down. A machine could do that easily. Instead, birds move their wings in complex ways to take off, turn, speed up, slow down, and land.

Looking at birds and planes, you can tell there are differences in design. Planes have vertical tails. Birds don't. Vertical tails reduce the side-to-side motion of the plane called **yaw**. Birds need to control yaw, too, but they manage without having a tail sticking up. Birds manage by changing the shape of their wings, tails, and bodies in ways way too complex for rigid-hulled airplanes to mimic.

Birds are like humans in that the bodies are supported by an internal structure of bones—a skeleton. Early airplanes used this same approach. Later, when stronger materials like aluminum were tried, designers went to the insect design approach: a hard exoskeleton. Like bugs, planes today have a rigid shell on the outside that supports all the stuff on the inside.

FLAPPING THE WINGS   Although airplanes don't flap their wings to fly, their wings do flap up and down during flight. The wing tips on a 747 can flex as much as nine feet, much farther than any bird.

FAMOUS FLIGHT LOGS

> ## First Flight Across the United States

Not fast by today's standards, but in 1911 pilot Calbraith Rodgers crossed the country in a plane. It took him 84 days, although his actual flying time was only three days and ten hours. By the time he reached the West coast, he had landed or crashed his plane about 70 times, and had to replace almost every part in his Wright airplane.

HUMAN-POWERED FLIGHT IS POSSIBLE

Inventor Paul MacCready and bicyclist Bryan Allen proved that in 1977 with the Gossamer Condor, and again in 1979 with the Gossamer Albatross. But MacCready's planes didn't flap their wings. They used propellers turned by a bicycle-like mechanism. Bryan Allen pedaled the planes. Even though they worked, they required the stamina of a competitive bicyclist and the strongest and lightest materials of the space age.

The earliest attempts to fly used human power, not engines. The idea was to attach wings to a person's arms and have him flap like crazy. But there is a fundamental problem with that. Birds can produce about ten times as much mechanical power per pound of muscle as humans. Or in engineering terms, the strength-to-weight ratio for humans is too low to fly. Even when people replaced muscle power with engine power in ornithopters, they weren't successful.

Inventing the Airplane

Orville and Wilbur Wright started a business in 1892 to build and sell what many people were calling one of the world's great inventions: bicycles. Seven years earlier J.K. Starley, an English bike maker, had invented the safety bicycle. It was a big improvement on the existing high-wheeler bikes that had huge front wheels (as tall as 5 feet, 1.5 meters) and tiny rear wheels. A few years later bike manufacturers started using air-filled tires. These two innovations sparked a surge in biking and bike sales. The Wright brothers took up riding and learned how to repair their own bikes. Soon people in Dayton, Ohio, were asking them to fix their bikes, so the Wright brothers decided to go into the bicycle business. At first, they found it difficult to make money, as there were thirteen other bike shops in Dayton.

By 1895 the Wright brothers were designing and building their own bicycles. People liked their bikes, and their business improved enough so they could save some money. Meanwhile, they had developed skills in working with wood and metal. With a life-long interest in flying, they used their profits to buy materials and their skills to build kites, gliders, and the world's first airplane.

GEO-SMART

All of the mountains in the United States that exceed 14,000 feet in elevation are found in just four states. Can you name them?

The tallest mountains in the United States are in Alaska, California, Colorado, and Washington.

The Challenge of Flight

The two problems facing airplane inventors were, first, how to get enough power, and second, how to control turns. The power problem was solved when two Germans, Gottlieb Daimler and Karl Benz, each invented the gasoline engine in 1885. These inventors later joined forces to create one of the world's first car manufacturing companies, Daimler-Benz, which made the first Mercedes.

The Wright brothers solved the second problem. From their experiences with bicycles, the Wrights figured out that, to turn a plane, the pilot couldn't just steer in the new direction like you steer a wagon. Flying a plane is similar to riding a bike: To turn, you have to *lean* into the turn. Their genius was in recognizing the problem and finding a solution.

Plane Smart

➤ Why Bi-Planes?

Why did early airplanes have two wings? To get enough lift, the planes needed large wings, but the materials available weren't strong enough to support wings stretching far from the fuselage. Using two wings instead of one allowed the wings to be half as long, and the two wings could be braced with wires to make them stronger.

As stronger materials and more powerful engines became available, plane builders started making **monoplanes** with one wing. Monoplanes can fly faster than bi-planes since they provide less resistance to air.

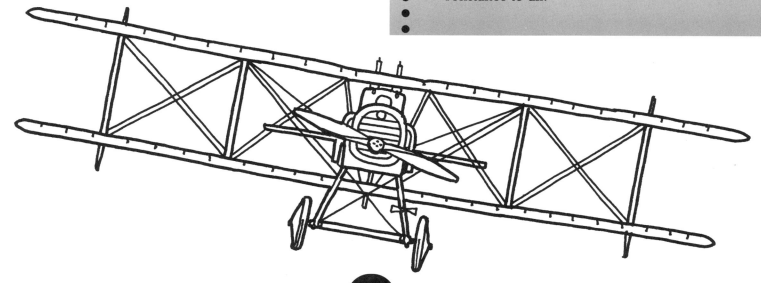

The Wright brothers created a simple control that let the pilot "lean" the airplane into a turn. When the pilot shifted his weight to make a turn, the motion bent the wings. To turn left, the right wing bent down to gain lift and the left wing bent up to lose lift. This bending of the wings, called *wing warping*, rolled the plane in the direction of the turn. Although wing warping worked, another great inventor discovered a better way to roll the plane.

THE WRIGHT'S ENGINE

The Wright's airplane, the "Flyer," had a twelve-horsepower engine. Today, riding lawn mowers have twelve-horsepower engines. The materials for the Wright Flyer cost less than $1,000. Using the value of a dollar today, the cost would be around $14,000.

THE FIRST FLIGHT

The Wright brothers succeeded in their quest to fly on December 17, 1903, at Kill Devil Hill, near Kitty Hawk on the outer banks of North Carolina. The first flight was about twelve seconds and 120 feet long. Orville piloted the first flight, but Wilbur had the longest flight of the day, 852 feet.

Speed Demon

Glenn Curtiss was a speed demon who raced bicycles and motorcycles. In 1903 Curtiss won the American motorcycle championship, setting the speed record for motorcycles at 64.5 miles per hour. In 1907 he designed and built a seven-foot-long motorcycle powered by an eight-cylinder engine. Riding this monster cycle, he established a world speed record at 136.3 miles per hour. At the time, nothing made by humans could go faster than Curtiss's motorcycle. He was still inventing improvements for motorcycles when he ventured into making engines for airplanes.

Curtiss made engines for **dirigibles**, lighter-than-air aircraft with hard bodies, and teamed up with Alexander Graham Bell (the famous inventor) to

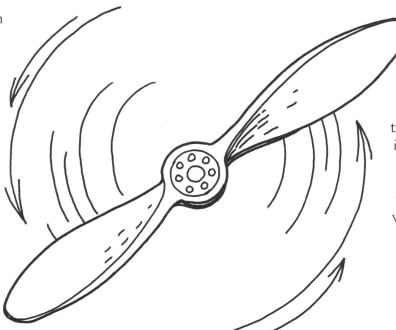

work on the airplane. To avoid infringing on the Wright brothers' patent for wing warping, Bell suggested that Curtiss install flaps on the end of the wings to control turns. (Necessity is the mother of invention.) These flaps proved to be a much better solution than wing warping. We call these flaps "ailerons," after the French word for a movable surface.

WHAT COULD BE LIGHTER THAN AIR?

Air is so light that a glass full of it seems empty. But there are things lighter still. Some balloons are filled with helium, which is lighter, or less dense, than air. Tie enough helium balloons together and you could lift a car. (We don't recommend that you do this.)

FAMOUS FLIGHT LOGS

➤ Smallest Plane

With wings spanning only five-and-a-half feet, the Bumble Bee is the smallest airplane to fly. Robert Starr first flew it in 1984.

Plane Smart

➤ The Most Successful Commercial Aircraft

There were more DC-3s built than any other aircraft. A total of 10,926 were produced starting in 1935. By the start of the World War II, 80% of commercial airplanes were DC-3s. DC stands for "Douglas Commercial," and the numbers that follow it indicate the model from DC-1 to DC-10.

In 1907, Curtiss won the trophy sponsored by *Scientific American* magazine for the first flight of one kilometer. Although the Wright bothers had invented the airplane, they had been too busy developing planes for the army to pursue the *Scientific American* competition. But after Curtiss won the trophy, the Wright Brothers claimed that the ailerons on his plane infringed on their patent, and they started a long legal battle. Their dispute was never fully resolved. Eventually, after Wilbur Wright had died in an accident, Orville Wright had retired, and Glenn Curtiss had given up control of his company, the two aircraft companies merged.

The Mail Connection

The earliest airline companies got started hauling mail. One of these was the All American Aviation company, which later grew into US Airways. To pick up mail in the Allegheny Mountain region of Pennsylvania and West Virginia, All American Aviation employees hung mail bags on poles so their planes could fly overhead and grab the bags with a hook. Talk about airmail!

CROP DUSTERS   Maybe the most unusual take-off for an airline was Delta's. It began in 1925 as the world's first crop dusting company. Four years later, the company started carrying passengers and, through mergers and acquisitions, grew to be one of the giants of the airline business.

Crop dusters fly eight to ten feet above fields to spray them with seeds, fertilizer, or pesticide. Pilots have to watch for telephone and electrical wires, utility towers, and other obstacles while they fly and spray the fields. They rely on satellite navigation systems to make sure they spray each row once and don't miss any.

Plane Smart

➤ Airmail
Today, in addition to airmail, airplanes carry nearly all first-class mail going farther than 200 miles

Airmail Service Takes Off

In 1918 President Wilson watched the first US Army airmail plane take off from Washington, D.C. on its way to Philadelphia. Unfortunately, the pilot had neither navigational equipment nor a sense of direction, and he ended up landing farther from Philadelphia than where he started in Washington!

After that, the Army carried airmail for only a few months. Then the US Post Office assumed responsibility and hired their own pilots. But they, too, had difficulty finding their way. When lost, pilots would fly low to look for a water tower that had a town's name painted on the side. After they experienced too many crashes, the Post Office, in 1926, contracted with commercial airplanes to fly the mail.

THE FIRST US AIRLINE
Tony Jannus piloted a flying boat between St. Petersburg and Tampa in 1914 to start the country's first regularly scheduled airline service. The plane had room for one passenger, who paid $5.00 for the 22-mile trip.

FIRST TRANSCONTINENTAL SERVICE
In 1930 TWA offered the first flights across the country, from New York to Los Angles. Passengers spent one night in Kansas City and continued the following day. It took 36 hours to cross the country. Today you can fly from New York to Los Angles in six hours.

May I Help You?

When airlines got started, there were no flight attendants and little or no service on board. By the 1920s, airlines recognized the need for in-flight service, so they hired men. Later, airlines eliminated these jobs to save money, and it wasn't until 1939 that airlines hired women as flight attendants. By then they had learned that women were as able as men to handle the rigors of being a flight attendant. For many years only women held flight attendant positions, but now airlines hire both men and women.

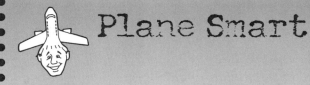

Plane Smart

➤ Live Entertainment

In your seat you probably can listen to a dozen channels of music, and if you're on a transcontinental flight you probably can watch a movie. But instead of recorded sounds or video, can you imagine having live entertainment on your flight?

Aluminum pianos provided the first entertainment on an airline. The Zeppelins carried pianos to keep passengers entertained during the long flights. More recently, Virgin Atlantic Airline gave free tickets to performers who would do their act during flights. Maybe you should work on a juggling or comedy routine and see if an airline will fly you for free.

3 FLYING

∙∙

Imagine you're an alien arriving on Earth after a long space journey from your home planet, Zenon. As you peer out your window, what catches your eye? What features of the land and water below you are the most dramatic?

Can you see the straight lines of roads? How about cities and towns? Can you see snow-covered peaks? Rock slides? Rivers or coastlines? If you were going to write the Zenon Traveler's Guide to Earth, how would you describe the things you see below? Add this to your Flight Log.

Hey, Who's Flying This Thing?

Computers, maybe. A cyber team of 140 microprocessors flies each 767. The computers can fly it automatically from takeoff to landing.

Today we rely on instruments to guide pilots, especially in bad weather. Before these instruments were invented, pilots flew by a set of rules called *VFR*, visual flight rules. These rules tell pilots when and where they can take off, fly, and land based on their ability to see other planes or obstacles. Pilots still use VFR in clear weather when they don't need instruments.

GEO-SMART

Which of the five Great Lakes lies entirely within the US?

Only Lake Michigan lies entirely within the US.

FLYING BY INSTRUMENTS How would you have felt being the first person to fly a plane without looking out the window to see where you were going? In 1929, General Jimmy Doolittle was the first person to do that. For fifteen minutes he piloted his plane by looking only at the instruments. He did this to prove that flying by instruments was possible. General Doolittle continued his aviation career and became a hero in World War II.

What's Holding Us Up?

Rocks fall. Why don't planes? Engines pull or push the plane through the air, but they don't get it into the air. Put a jet engine on a car and you get a jet car, not a plane. And you get a pretty scary ride to the grocery store.

It's the wings that hold up the plane. Somehow it doesn't seem possible that two metal wings sticking out to the sides of a plane keep it flying, but they do. The magic of wings is that air flowing over top has to travel farther than air flowing under them. Check out the shape of the wings on your plane. The bottom is flat and the top is bowed upward. Separating two molecules of air at the front of the wing and sending one over the top and the other underneath, with instructions to meet up at the trailing edge, makes the "over the top" molecule travel faster. Since it has farther to travel, it has to go faster. Faster moving **fluids**, liquids and gases, have lower pressure, so the wing has lower pressure on the top than on the bottom. If you flow enough air fast enough over the top of the wing, you'll get it to rise. You're flying.

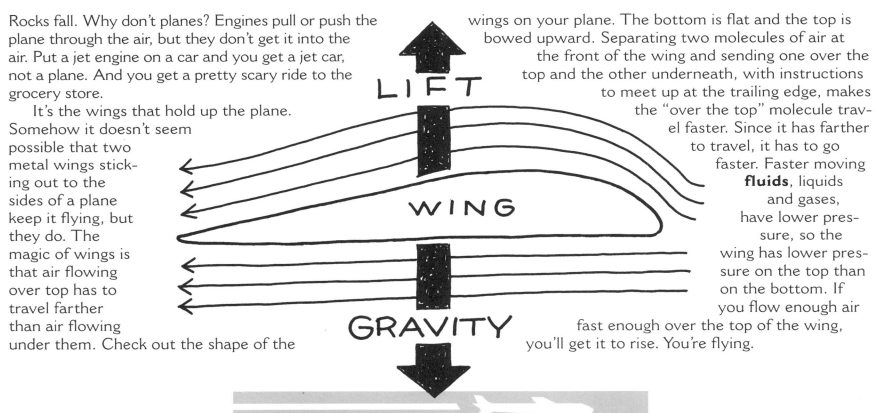

LIFT

WING

GRAVITY

FREQUENT FLYER AWARD   We give the frequent flyer award to the bee. To produce one tablespoon of honey, a bee makes 4,200 trips to flowers and back to the hive.

Get a Lift

Rip a strip of paper from the in-flight magazine four inches long and an inch wide. Now hold one end of the strip between the thumb and forefinger of each hand in front of your lips. What do you think will happen when you blow hard across the top of the paper?

You might think that your breath will bend the paper even lower. But instead, it rises. The faster moving air exerts lower pressure above the paper, causing it to rise. In planes, the shape of the wings causes the air to move faster across the top of the wing, and this faster moving air pulls the plane up.

DID YOU SAY ROPES? Inventors before the Wright brothers hadn't figured out that airplanes have to roll to turn. The Wright brothers invented a way to roll the plane, but their method was to bend the wings by pulling on them with a system of ropes.

The upward force that keeps the plane, a bird, or Frisbee® in the air is called **lift**. Lift opposes the gravity that is constantly tugging downward on things. To get more lift, designers can increase the size of the wings or increase the speed of the plane. The faster a plane goes, the more lift its wings generate.

When birds get going really fast, they don't need as much lift so they actually decrease the area of their wings, by scrunching them down. Airliners increase the wing area to generate more lift for take-offs and landings, but as the plane's speed increases, generating more lift, the pilot retracts the wing extensions, like birds.

Flying High

Cruising altitude for most jet flights is around 33,000 feet to 40,000 feet. Why so high?

Pilots fly jets where they are cheapest to operate, because that's how airlines make money. Planes can go faster at high altitudes, where there is less drag and colder air allows engines to run more efficiently.

At high altitudes, the air is much thinner (has lower density), and thinner air gives both less drag and less lift. The lower drag saves fuel, so that's good. The loss of lift due to lower air density is offset by the gain in lift due to the higher plane speed.

A plane flying at lower altitudes, where it encounters denser air, will generate more lift. If it makes too much lift, either the plane gains altitude or the pilot has to fly at a slower speed. Slower speed means longer flights for you and lower profits for the airline.

Plane Smart

➤ Don't Be Fuelish

A 747 burns about 22,000 pounds of fuel each hour its in flight. That's about 4% of the total weight of the aircraft. So, each hour it's flying, a 747 burns 4% of its weight. That's about the same rate at which a hummingbird burns its fuel. However, a hummingbird, being just a bit smaller than a 747, uses only 0.09 ounces per hour.

There are other benefits to flying high. Look out the window. If there are clouds in the sky, they're all below you. You are flying above thunderstorms, rain, sleet, and all the other messy stuff. That makes the pilot's job easier and your ride more comfortable.

HEY, IT'S COLD OUTSIDE

As your plane climbs, the outside air temperature drops. As an estimate, you can assume the temperature drops about 3.5°F for every 1,000 feet of elevation. So at 30,000 feet the air temperature could be 100°F colder than at sea level. Aren't you glad you're sitting inside the plane and not outside on the wing?

> ## Gliders

How far do you suppose a glider can glide? The record is about 907.7 miles. Hans Grosse flew his sailplane that distance in 1972.

Turn Off the Engines

If you turned off the engines, how far could your plane glide? Let's say you are cruising at 30,000 feet and you shut off all the engines. Your plane will fall one foot for every 15 feet it glides, so your plane could glide 85 miles.

The 15 feet of gliding for every foot of falling is called the **glide ratio**. Each type of plane, bird, and flying bug has its own glide ratio. The largest glide ratios are for sailplanes. They can sail as far as 40 feet for every foot dropped. Engineers would say that sailplanes have a 40:1 glide ratio.

Soaring birds, like the albatross, have a ratio as high as 20:1. They can fly for days without resting. Birds that don't fly

OPEN YOUR WINDOW Did you notice that your window doesn't open? Believe it or not, until 1930 airliners had windows that opened. But as planes started flying at higher altitudes, cabins were pressurized, which meant that the windows had to be sealed. Pressurizing means that the air pressure inside is kept higher than the pressure outside. People have a hard time breathing at altitudes above 15,000 feet, so flying at 30,000 feet would be a problem unless the cabin were pressurized.

well or far, like the pheasant, have low glide ratios, less than 5:1. But they don't need to glide. They take to the air only briefly to escape a predator and then land in another part of the corn field.

FAMOUS FLIGHT LOGS

> ### Amelia Earhart

In 1927 Amelia Earhart was the first woman to fly cross the Atlantic Ocean. Five years later, she was the first woman to fly solo and nonstop across the Atlantic. She was also the first woman to be awarded the Distinguished Flying Cross and the first person to fly solo from Hawaii to California. With her navigator, Fred Noonan, Earhart disappeared trying to fly around the world in 1937. No one has ever found a trace of Earhart, Noonan, or their plane, and what happened to them remains an unsolved mystery.

Flying Without a Plane

The first flight machine was a hot air balloon designed by the Montgolfier brothers in 1783. Once they demonstrated that balloon flight was possible, other people started making and flying balloons.

Balloons are fun, but they aren't practical for transportation. You travel whatever direction the wind is blowing, regardless of where you want to go.

But what if you attach an engine to a balloon? That seems like a neat idea, only a ball-shaped balloon isn't easy to push through the air. If you made the balloon into a sausage shape, it could work better. And it did. People call these flying sausages **blimps**.

FAMOUS FLIGHT LOGS

> ## HISTORY HIGHLIGHT: FIRST TO CROSS THE ATLANTIC OCEAN

No, it wasn't Charles Lindbergh. Lindbergh was the first to cross the ocean nonstop and alone. During May 20-21, 1927, Lindbergh soloed across the Atlantic and captured the imagination and hearts of people around the world. He also won a $25,000 prize for being the first person to fly nonstop from New York to Paris.

To pay for an airplane capable of crossing the ocean, Lindbergh appealed for financial backing to a group of nine businessmen from St. Louis. He named his plane the "Spirit of St. Louis" in their honor. It took Lindbergh 33.5 hours to cover the 3,600 miles. Today, you could fly that far in eight hours. So if Lindbergh wasn't the first to cross the Atlantic Ocean, who was? The honor goes to Albert C. Reed, who flew a Navy flying boat across in 1919. Three planes took off together in the attempt. The Navy had stationed twenty-one destroyers along the route stretching from Newfoundland to the Azores and Lisbon, Spain to pick up the planes should they fall in the ocean. Two of the planes dropped down below the clouds to find their position and landed on the ocean. Due to the heavy seas, neither was able to take off again. One sank, but the crew was saved by one of the destroyers. The other taxied across the water the remaining 200 miles to the Azores. Albert Reed, in the third plane, refueled in the Azores and continued on to Spain becoming the first pilot to fly across the Atlantic Ocean.

TRY THIS

Things With Wings

Can you figure out what these symbols might mean?

1.

2.

3.

4.

5.

6.

7.

8.

9.

10.

11.

12.

13.

14.

Answers: Things with wings

1. Flight school
2. Buffalo wings
3. Flying high
4. Flying blind
5. Air mail
6. Butterfly
7. Flypaper
8. Housefly
9. Flights of fancy
10. Flights of imagination
11. Air mattress
12. Airfield
13. Airship
14. Airhead

Plane Smart

➤ Weird Name

Where did the name "blimp" come from? There are two stories. One is that during World War I, the US Navy was using limp airships. The first model "limp" was type "A" and it didn't work out well. The second model, "B" limp, worked much better and came to be called the blimp.

Others say instead that Lt. Cunningham of the British Royal Navy Air Service flicked his thumb on the side of a blimp in 1915. When he heard the distinctive sound, he mimicked it with a word which came out as "blimp."

Making Your Own Blimp

When you attend a birthday party, save a helium-filled balloon. When you get it home, add some weight to the string so it neither rises or falls when you let it go. Paper clips work great. Now, can you make a propeller and a gizmo to turn the propeller? You could use a small, battery-powered electric motor, or a rubber band. Maybe you can hook together several balloons to make a multi-blimp.

BAGS OF WIND

Blimps are bags of light gas with a gondola and engines attached. There are no support structures inside the gas bags; gas fills the bags like an inflated balloon. The gondola houses the crew and passengers underneath the blimp.

THE FIRST COMMERCIAL AIRLINE

The first commercial airline didn't operate airplanes; it used airships. In 1909 Count Ferdinand von Zeppelin started the first airline, called DELAG. The first airship was the 485 foot (148 meters) long *Deutschland*. In four years of operation, DELAG carried more than 10,000 passengers.

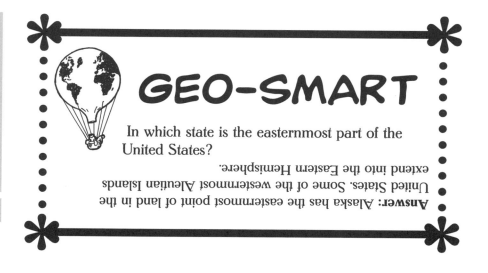

GEO-SMART

In which state is the easternmost part of the United States?

Answer: Alaska has the easternmost point of land in the United States. Some of the westernmost Aleutian Islands extend into the Eastern Hemisphere.

Another type of airship is the **dirigible** or Zeppelin. These were giants, as long 800 feet (244 meters). Unlike blimps, which are gas-filled balloons, Zeppelins had an internal structure supporting the skin. Zeppelins were like birds whose bones support the weight, while blimps are like bugs without bones, with the skin itself maintaining the shape.

In both blimps and Zeppelins, the gas inside is lighter (less dense) than air outside. Airships float in air like ships float in water. Engines that propel airships can be relatively small since they don't need to move the ship fast enough to generate lift.

Cloud Nine

One of the great things about flying in a jet airplane is getting above the clouds.

Except for cirrus clouds, most clouds are below 20,000 feet, and since jets normally cruise above 30,000 feet, you generally fly in clear skies.

Does the sky seem bluer at high altitudes than from ground? It is. Gas molecules and microscopic particles in the air scatter sunlight, giving the sky color. Without this scattering, the sky would look black. But why does the sky look blue?

Different sizes of particles scatter different wavelengths of light. That's why a dust storm or volcanic eruption can give spectacular sunsets. Those dust-sized particles scatter red light, so we see the red color. In the atmosphere, unless there is a lot of dust or pollution, violet and blue light are scattered the most, so we see a blue sky. Our eyes are more sensitive to blue, so although violet light is scattered even more than blue, the sky looks blue to us.

LINDBERGH'S LEGACY Although he was the 79th person to cross the Atlantic Ocean by air, Lindbergh captured the attention of the country with his transatlantic flight in 1927 and forever changed the way we travel. In the year of his flight, there were only thirty commercial airplanes in America. Three years later the industry included thirty-eight American *airlines*.

Contrails

On some days you can see **contrails** crisscrossing the sky. Other days there are none. Why?

Contrails means "condensation trails." These are trails of water vapor that have condensed into water droplets or frozen as ice crystals. The water comes from the fuel burning in airplane engines. On days when the air is both cool and moist, contrails can form as air mixes with airplane exhaust gases. If the air is warm and dry, you are less likely to see contrails.

Look For Contrails

Your car can make contrails on cold mornings. Look for the white plume coming from your exhaust pipe when you're first starting out. After a few minutes, as the engine heats up, the contrail will disappear.

While you're in the air you can see other condensation trails. Where? One place is an inch above the surface of a cup of hot coffee. And, when the plane is landing, look for white plumes spewing off the top of the wing. The lower pressure on the top of the wing causes moist air to condense and form contrails.

Make A Contrail

If you have a teapot at home, ask if you can heat up some water. When the water boils, you will be making a stream of condensation. The hot, moist air coming out of the pot will mix with the cooler air above it. When the two mix, some of the water vapor condenses.

Meal Time

At the airport, as we've seen, trays of food are loaded into the food service carts the flight attendants push up and down the aisles. The carts are locked into storage spaces in the galley. Since planes use a lot of nautical terms, everyone calls the kitchen the "galley," like they do aboard a ship.

Some of the carts used on planes have heating elements built into them. Flight attendants plug the carts into electrical outlets to heat the food. When your meal arrives, feel the bottom of the tray. Is the entire tray hot, or just one side? In most cases, one side will be hot and the other will be cold. Why?

The heating elements in the cart contact only one side of each food tray. The kitchen staff are careful to load the entrees that need to be warmed on the side of the cart that has the heating elements. The other side stays cold for salads and desserts.

HOW MUCH FOOD IS ENOUGH? Aboard a 747, the galley crew has five and a half tons of food and supplies. Maybe you should ask for seconds!

The Ultimate Dream: The Rocket Belt

Consider this: You strap on a rocket belt and jet over to your friend's house. The good news is that rocket belts have actually been invented.

The bad news? The Army got interested in rocket belts in the early 1950s

as a way to help soldiers get over obstacles or observe an enemy from above the battlefield. The first tethered flight was made in 1958 and, three years later, engineer Harold Graham made the first free flight in a rocket belt. Since then, engineers have made many improvements to it, but it still doesn't work well enough. Although the rocket belt can lift people off the ground, it can't carry them far, and the cost is high.

Today rocket belts are used occasionally in movies, but nowhere else.

FAMOUS FLIGHT LOGS

➤ **First Supersonic Flight**

General Chuck Yeager was the first to fly faster than the speed of sound. In 1947 Yeager piloted a Bell XS-1 aircraft at 670 miles per hour (1081 kilometers per hour). Yeager was racing horses the night before his historic flight, and fell off, cracking his ribs. Knowing that if he reported his injury he wouldn't be allowed to fly, he kept it secret, flew the plane, and broke the sound barriers. His exploits became one of the central stories in the book and movie, **The Right Stuff**.

GEO-SMART

Which four states touch at one point?

Answer: The four corner states are Colorado, Utah, New Mexico, and Arizona.

The Black Box

Everything on your airplane has undergone vigorous testing. But the toughest testing of all is reserved for the black box.

The black box keeps a record of the thrust generated by each engine, the angles of flaps, altitude, position of the landing gear, velocity, acceleration, and voices of the pilot and co-pilot. In case of an accident, officials at the National Transportation Safety Board can play back the tape to figure out what went wrong.

The black box must withstand being shot from a cannon into a target at 3,400 times the force of gravity (G). Most people would pass out if subjected to just two or three Gs. Then the box is stabbed with a steel rod. Did we mention that the steel rod is dropped from a height of ten feet, and that it has a 500-pound weight attached to it? Then the box goes to the compression test, where engineers squeeze it with a vise to 5,000 pounds of pressure. After that, they torture it with blow torches at 1,900° F. Then they bake it at 470° F for ten hours before trying to drown it in sea water for a month at the pressure equivalent of 20,000 feet (6,098 meters). Superman would be hard pressed to survive all that. But the black box does.

THE ORANGE BOX? It's odd that everyone calls it the black box, because it's orange. Black would make it harder to find. The whole apparatus is just a few inches longer than a toaster oven but includes a steel shell, insulation, a layer of wax to protect it against heat, and a magnetic recorder.

4 WHERE ARE WE?

When people first started flying, it was tough to find their way. There were no navigational aids to help them, and they couldn't pull over to ask someone at a gas station for directions. Pilots had to recognize and follow features along the ground like roads, streams, and mountain ranges. When clouds built up, there was no way to fly safely. So engineers and inventors started creating systems to help pilots navigate.

Finding Your Way

Can you find where you are on a map? First check out the in-flight magazine in the seat pocket ahead of you. If you don't find a map, ask the flight attendant if he can get one. Or use the map.

As you look out the window, see if you can identify major features. Lakes, major rivers, and coastlines are easy to see, as light shimmers off the surface. Reservoirs are easy to recognize because of the straight shoreline formed by a dam. Straight lines on the ground are roads. If you follow them with your eyes, you might see a town or city in the distance. Compare what you see out the window to what you expect to see in different locations along your route. This kind of navigation, finding your way by looking at the features on land is, called **pilotage**.

✪ ✪

GEO-SMART

Check out the map below. All the state boundaries are drawn, but not the state's names. Can you write in the names for all the states?
See the answers on page 88.

Invisible Highways

Today, pilots have several systems of navigation to help them find their way. Radio broadcasts are one. These aren't heavy metal or country stations, just a steady message of "here I am." There are hundreds of these **VOR** or very high frequency, omni-directional range radio stations across the country. A pilot tunes a radio to the frequency of a VOR station he wants and steers toward or away from the signal. The positions and frequencies of each VOR are shown on aeronautical maps so the pilot can select the ones he needs when making his flight plan. These electronic signals guide planes on the invisible highways of the sky.

FAMOUS FLIGHT LOGS

➤ First Around-the-World Flight

It wasn't speedy, but they made it. In 1924 four Navy torpedo planes flew around the world. With frequent stops for repairs and refueling, the circumnavigation took them **six months**.

Some planes have **inertial** navigation systems. These measure and record all the accelerations, or changes in speed, and use them to estimate the plane's velocity. If a strong gust of wind moves the plane to one side, the inertial navigation system records the acceleration and calculates the distance the plane was moved. By keeping track of all these tiny changes, it can calculate how far a plane has gone and what direction it has traveled to give the plane's position all the time.

The newest system uses satellites to provide navigation information. Twenty-four satellites surround the world and beam radio signals toward earth. The navigation system on the plane receives several of these signals and calculates precisely how far away the satellites are. The system, called **GPS** (for Global Positioning System), is so easy to use and so accurate that it is replacing the older systems. If you get to visit the flight deck, ask to see the navigation systems, especially the GPS.

In addition to the several navigation systems on board, air traffic controllers can track planes on their radar screens. Not only does their radar show that there is an airplane at your location, but it also shows your flight number and airline. To get this information onto the controller's screen, each plane sends a radio message identifying itself. This information appears on the controller's radar screen at the position of the plane so the controllers know which plane to call to pass on routing information.

With thousands of dollars of navigation equipment in the plane, you're less likely to get lost once you're flying than you are in finding your way to the airport.

Plane Smart

➤ Seadromes

Long before trans-oceanic flights became common, people suggested building seadromes, or airports floating in the ocean. Their idea was to manufacture a series of floating islands where airplanes could land and refuel. Seadromes would be outfitted with hotels and other services for passengers. They would be high enough above the water that storm waves wouldn't interfere with flight operations. Designs were made that showed a 1,200-foot-long landing platform with repair shops, hangars, and quarters for the crew and visitors below the platform. With modern jets able to fly across oceans, you will probably never see a seadrome. But the Navy has aircraft carriers that are floating islands in the ocean. And maybe we will build seadromes in outer space as fuel stations or rest stops for space ships.

How Fast Are You Going?

The pilot may announce how fast the plane is traveling. She may also give the wind speed and tell you whether the wind is pushing the plane faster or slowing it down.

Once you know the plane's speed, you can calculate how long it will take to arrive. The pilot will also announce the total distance between airports, or you could look it up in the airline's schedule or timetable. (If you don't have a schedule, ask a flight attendant for one.) Once you have the distance in either miles or kilometers and you have the plane's speed (make sure you use the same system of units for both distance and speed), you can calculate the time it should take. For example, if the distance to your destination is 900 miles and the plane is flying at an average speed of 450 miles per hour, flying time should be about 900 miles divided by 450 miles per hour, or 2 hours. See if your estimate for flight time is the same as the captain's. If it's not, can you figure out why there's a difference?

GEO-SMART

Many cities across the country have distinctive skylines, buildings, or historic features. Can you match the pictures with each of the following structures: Seattle's Space Needle, Golden Gate Bridge, Empire State Building, St. Louis Gateway Arch, San Antonio Alamo, Chicago Sears Tower, Orlando's EPCOT, Washington Monument, Philadelphia's Liberty Bell, Canton's Football Hall of Fame.

Answer: 1. EPCOT, 2. Gateway Arch, 3. Empire State Building, 4. Space Needle, 5. Washington Monument, 6. Liberty Bell, 7. Alamo, 8. Golden Gate Bridge, 9. Sears Tower, 10. Football Hall of Fame

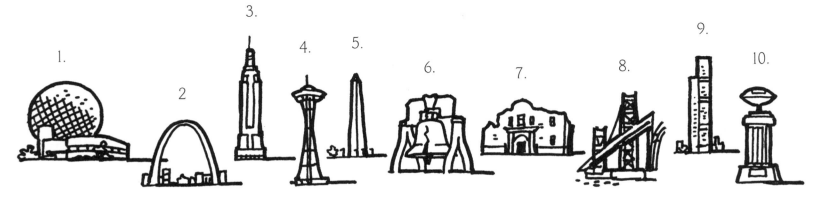

1. 2. 3. 4. 5. 6. 7. 8. 9. 10.

It's a Bird, It's a Plane. . .
It's Aerodynamics!

Across

3. Another word for air resistance
4. It surrounds the earth and moving things must pass through it
5. The smooth slim shape that allows things to move easily through the air

8. The upward force underneath the wing that keeps the plane in the air
10. It must be the right shape and at the right angle for the plane to stay in the air
12. The part of the plane made of the horizontal stabilizer and the vertical stabilizer
13. It spins in the front of some planes to make them go

Down

1. The last name of a woman pilot whose plane disappeared in 1937
2. Wilbur and Orville _ _ _ _ _ _. They built the first plane that had a motor and a propeller.
4. Movable flaps on the wing of an airplane
6. The force that slows down an object as it moves throught the air is called air _ _ _ _ _ _ _ _ _ _.
7. The flaps on the horizontal part of the tail that make the nose of the plane go up or down
9. The flap on the vertical part of the tail that helps turn the plane right or left
11. What humans have wanted to do ever since they saw a bird soar through the air
13. The person who flies the airplane

See the answers on page 87.

Reprinted with permission from *WonderScience*. Copyright 1990 by the American Chemical Society.

Flying East Is Faster

You travel faster going east because winds in the jet stream push you in that direction.

Ask the flight attendant for a copy of the airline timetable or see if there is a copy in one of the small racks on a bulkhead (that's plane talk for wall). Compare the flight times for two identical flights, one from an east coast airport heading west and the other going in the opposite direction. You'll find that it takes about a half hour longer to go west than it does to go east for a flight across the United States In making this comparison, make sure that the flight you picked doesn't stop along the way.

Where's the Airport?

Say you take off from St. Louis and head due south. The pilot tells you the winds are 30 miles per hour from the west. You fly for one hour at 400 miles per hour (speed through the air). Then, the pilot turns to the right and flies due west for one hour at the same throttle setting. After one hour on this heading, he turns north. At the end of one more hour, how far are you from the St. Louis airport? How long will it take you to get there?

Answers: After three hours of flying, you are 310 miles due west of the St. Louis airport. With no wind, you would have been 400 miles due west. With the 30-mile-per-hour wind blowing you toward the east for three hours, you have moved 90 miles to the east. If the jet continues to make 400 miles through the air, it will take you 43 minutes to get back. You have 310 miles to go at a speed of 430 miles per hour (adding the speed through the air and the speed of the air), which is 0.72 hours or a little over 43 minutes.

The Jet Stream

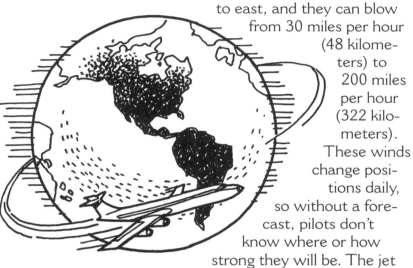

The jet stream is a band of winds found at high altitudes. Over North America these winds are generally from west to east, and they can blow from 30 miles per hour (48 kilometers) to 200 miles per hour (322 kilometers). These winds change positions daily, so without a forecast, pilots don't know where or how strong they will be. The jet stream coincides with the polar front, which separates the cold air coming from the polar region from the warmer air to the south. The boundary between the two air masses moves in a snake-like or wave pattern that television weather forecasters show during their reports. When the jet stream dips low into the upper mid-west during winter, you can be sure temperatures there will drop. Meteorologists predict the location of the jet stream so aircraft can avoid it (going west) or take advantage of it (going east).

FAMOUS FLIGHT LOGS

➤ The First Nonstop Transcontinental Flights

The first nonstop transcontinental flights were all one-way. In 1953 both TWA and American Airlines wanted to offer nonstop service between New York and Los Angeles. The prevailing winds allowed their DC-7s and Super Constellations to complete the trip from west to east without a stop, but not the other way. Flying from New York to Los Angeles, the planes had to stop in Chicago to refuel.

MOST EXPERIENCED PILOT Pilots measure their experience flying in hours. John Edward Long logged over 60,000 hours as a pilot before he retired. That's the equivalent of thirty years of work.

Time Zones

Flight attendants always announce the local time upon landing to remind you to set your watch forward or backward if you started in a different time zone. Some people get confused by time zones, but think of the mess before standard time zones. Each city and town set its clocks according to when the sun passed highest overhead. When the sun was at its zenith, the high point, it was noon. This time-keeping system works great if you interact only with people who live in the same city, but imagine trying to operate a railroad and give schedules when every town on the line kept its own time!

As railroads grew in the United States, they established more consistent time zones. These were called "railroad times." In 1863 there were about 100 different railroad times. That was still too confusing, so railroad officials decided to divide the country into four time zones. The following year, worldwide time zones were established. We call them Standard Times, as in the

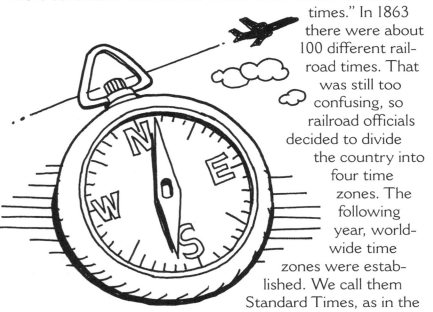

➤ First Nonstop Circumnavigation

It took three days and twenty-two hours for a United States Air Force crew to travel 23,452 miles (39,086 kilometers) around the world in 1949. They had to refuel in flight several times.

MAKING TIME In traveling from the east coast of the United States to the west you pass through four time zones, and you "gain" three hours. If your watch is set for east coast time in the United States, you will have to reset it three hours back to be on west coast time; when you land in Seattle you will have an extra three hours in your day. Returning to the east coast you will "lose" three hours.

Eastern Standard Time Zone. When we switch our watches in spring to create daylight savings time, we are deviating from the agreed standard, and we call the time zone the Eastern Daylight Savings Time.

The countries of the world have adopted time zone standards. Within a zone, everyone keeps the same time. Since there are twenty-four hours in a day, there are twenty-four time zones, plus a few more squeezed in among the other zones.

So if you keep traveling west, why don't you keep gaining time? As you continue westward and cross the International Date Line, you lose a day. That can be pretty confusing. If you fly from Japan to San Francisco, you can land before you take off. Time warp.

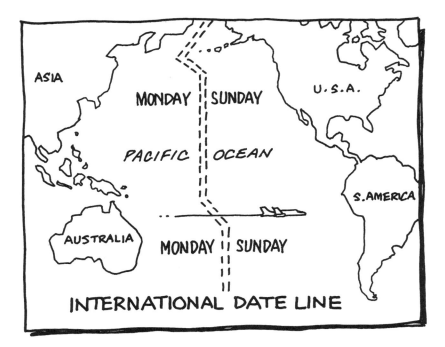

INTERNATIONAL DATE LINE

ZONED OUT   There are some exceptions to the general rules about time zones. In the United States, not all the states go on daylight savings time. Arizona has decided not to adopt it. A few countries have time zones one half hour off from what you'd expect. The people of Alaska have decided, even though their state spans four time zones, to have the entire state on one zone. And, the International Date Line, zigs and zags around Alaska to keep it entirely in the same day. Otherwise, what a mess that would be: If someone was going to call you from Alaska on a particular date, you'd have to ask them from what part of the state they would be calling to know when to expect the call.

Plane Smart

➤ How Wide Is an Hour?

Since the earth spins once in twenty-four hours, and since there are 360° around a circle (the earth), the earth spins 15° each hour (360 divided by 24). So, each of the twenty-four time zones is 15° wide.

Jet Lag

People traveling across the country in a Connestoga wagon may have lost all their possessions crossing a river, run out of food, and had to repair broken axles and wheels, but they didn't suffer jet lag. If you travel east or west at 500 miles an hour, jet lag will hit. You'll know it because you'll be tired but *unable to fall asleep*.

Jet lag has nothing to do with jets. But jet engines make rapid air travel possible, and that makes people aware of the natural rhythms of the human body. If you travel through more than one or two time zones in a day, your body's natural clock and cycles, called the **circadian rhythm**, are disrupted. (The word "circadian" comes from Latin and means "about a day.") Your circadian rhythms are tuned to your rest and active periods. If you fly from Atlanta to Seattle, even though you set your watch to Seattle time, your body remains on Atlanta time for a few days. When Seattle people are ready to eat dinner, you will be ready to go to bed. You might think that shortening your day by flying east from Seattle to Atlanta would be easier, but it isn't. At home, your routine of waking and sleeping and the pattern of daylight and nightfall keeps your circadian rhythm attuned to the twenty-four-hour cycle we call a day. When you skip these cues, your rhythm stretches out closer to twenty-five hours. So when you travel east, your body wants to add an extra hour to the day, but you are cutting three hours out of it. That's a four-hour impact to your internal clock. Traveling to the west coast isn't as bad because as your body wants to add an extra hour, your time zone change is adding three. So the impact is only a two-hour change.

WHAT TO DO ABOUT JET LAG

Although there is no known cure or prevention for jet lag, you can try some things that may help.

- On short trips, don't try to change to the new time zone. Just sleep and eat as you would at home. (But this only works if everyone can accommodate your schedule.)

- Ease your way into the new time zone. For example, if you're going to fly from Seattle to Atlanta, start changing your cycles two or three days before your trip. You could get up one hour earlier the first day and then go to bed an hour earlier that night, and then get up an additional hour earlier the second morning.

- The sleep cycle isn't the only one that determines your circadian rhythm. Food and sunlight also help set your internal clocks. Protein resets your clock to morning, and eating it at the right time can help you adjust. For example, eating a protein-based breakfast on board the plane could help reset your rhythm to the new time zone while flying west. Following the same strategy going east could make your jet lag much worse. In that case, the protein would tell your body that it was morning when in your new time zone people would be ready for lunch.

- Getting exercise and exposure to daylight at your destination will help you adjust to a new time zone.

Can you match the states with their nicknames, state birds, products, or flowers?

State

_____Alabama	_____Kentucky	_____North Dakota
_____Alaska	_____Louisiana	_____Ohio
_____Arizona	_____Maine	_____Oklahoma
_____Arkansas	_____Maryland	_____Oregon
_____California	_____Massachusetts	_____Pennsylvania
_____Colorado	_____Michigan	_____Rhode Island
_____Connecticut	_____Minnesota	_____South Carolina
_____Delaware	_____Mississippi	_____South Dakota
_____Florida	_____Missouri	_____Tennessee
_____Georgia	_____Montana	_____Texas
_____Hawaii	_____Nebraska	_____Utah
_____Idaho	_____Nevada	_____Vermont
_____Illinois	_____New Hampshire	_____Virginia
_____Indiana	_____New Jersey	_____Washington
_____Iowa	_____New Mexico	_____West Virginia
_____Kansas	_____New York	_____Wisconsin
	_____North Carolina	_____Wyoming

Identification

1. Named after an island in England
2. State name was derived from the Spanish word for "red"
3. The "keystone" state
4. State name means "land of the Indians"
5. This state broke away from another state that was trying to break away from the United States
6. The "Pelican State"
7. Extends farthest north of the 48 contiguous states
8. State name is derived from French meaning green mountain
9. This state bird prefers running to flying
10. The largest New England state
11. The northern border of this state was the Mason-Dixon Line
12. This is the fourth largest state in area
13. Part of the Great American Desert
14. Home of the tallest mountain in New England
15. Means "snow-clad" in Spanish
16. Where the Civil War started
17. The only state that has coastlines along

the Great Lakes and Atlantic Ocean

18. Where Orville and Wilbur made history
19. Only state in the continental US that has sections (not islands) entirely separated by water
20. Home of the "cheese heads"
21. Nicknamed for people who sneak in early to claim the best lands
22. Home of Mt. Rushmore
23. The first of these United States
24. The "Ocean State"
25. Home of Bryce Canyon National Park
26. This state was briefly a separate country
27. Lowest population of any state
28. "The Gem State"
29. The "volunteer" state
30. Home of eight US presidents
31. This state was name by Ponce de Leon during his search for the Fountain of Youth
32. Home to inventors Thomas Edison, the Wright Brothers, and Charles Kettering
33. The Beaver State
34. Only state named for a U.S. president
35. This state was once a kingdom
36. Stephen Douglas debated Abraham Lincoln here
37. Home of the country's most famous tea party

38. State motto is "Eureka"
39. The Lewis and Clark Expedition started here
40. The only state that has two land areas separated by water
41. The state of Mocking Birds and Magnolias
42. State song is "Home on the Range"
43. State name derived from Mohican word for "long river place"
44. The state bird is the Willow ptarmigan
45. Ozark Mountains are found here
46. 93% of the land in this state is farms
47. Home to the most famous horse race
48. Often has the coldest spot in the US in winter
49. Has a cactus as the state flower
50. General Sherman marched to the sea through this state

See the answers on page 89.

TRY THIS

Let Your Creativity Take Wings

What can you make out of the materials you have at hand? In the seat pocket ahead of you is an airsick bag. Can you make a puppet out of it? How about turning the top edge down to make a basket for a tiny game of basketball? What can you use for a ball? How about a crumpled-up piece of paper?

Do you have earphones? What happens when you pinch one of the tubes while listening to the movie or music? Try pinching one of the tubes, then the other, and then both.

Can you whisper in one end of the earphones so the person wearing them can hear you? Can you use them like a doctor's stethoscope to listen to your heart?

How many uses can you come up with for the stuff you find in the seat pocket? Have a contest with someone to see who can write down the longest list of uses for them.

JUST TO STRING YOU ALONG If you laid out the wire in a 737, it would stretch over 40 miles (67 kilometers). A 757 has even more: 60 miles of wire (100 kilometers).

40 MILES

5 DESIGNING YOUR OWN PLANE

Are you next in the line of great airplane designers: Boeing, Lockheed, Martin, Douglas, and you? Here's your chance. Grab a piece of paper—even a napkin will do—and start designing.

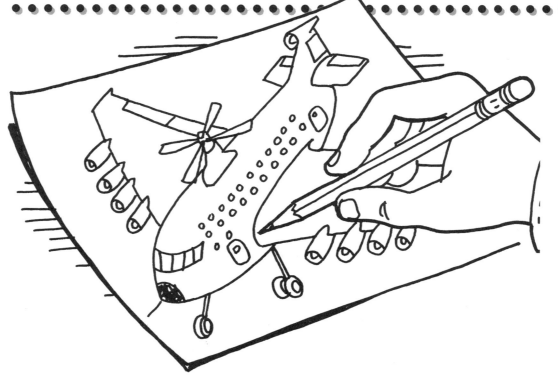

FAMOUS FLIGHT LOGS

> ## First Transatlantic Service

Pan Am was the first airline to offer transatlantic plane service in 1939. Instead of using airplanes, they used flying boats so they could land in the water if they had an engine problem. It wasn't until after World War II that Pan Am started using airplanes in place of the slower flying boats.

First, think about these questions.

- **How many people and how much cargo do you want to haul?** Will your plane be one size larger than the 747? Or will you design it for only yourself and a few friends?

- **How will you get passengers to their seats?** Can you design super large doors and hatches to let more people in at a time? Can you make it faster for the ground crew to bring on food and clean the plane?

- **How many aisles will you have?** Each additional aisle makes it easier for passengers to move around, but each one takes up room that could be filled with seats. How many seats will you put together in a row?

- **What entertainment features do you want to include?** A video system? How about a cable system so each passenger has choices of what video they watch?

Where will you put the video screens? Will you offer electronic games? How about having computer terminals so people can work or play at their seat? A phone for every passenger?

CHICKEN NUGGETS One of the many tests new engines have to pass is the "chicken test." A cannon shoots a four-pound chicken body into the engine while it is operating at full speed. The test is conducted to imitate colliding with a large bird.

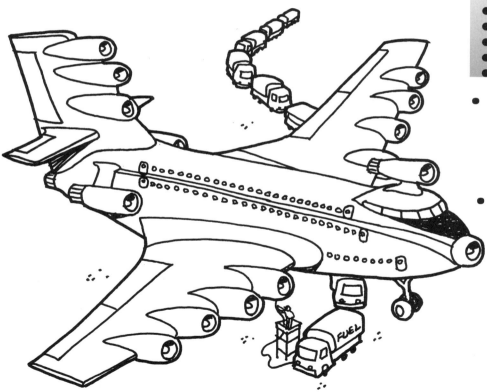

- **How about solving the storage problem?** People always carry an armful of packages to cram into the overhead storage compartments. How can you provide more storage room? Could passengers store bags in below-deck lockers underneath their feet?

- **How many engines will your plane have?** Two engines are okay for a small plane. But if you're moving lots of people and providing them specialized entertainment systems, you may need four or more engines.

- **Does your plane need long, graceful wings?** Large wings provide more lift, but they also provide more drag at high speeds. Can you have wings that change their size or shape depending on the speed? (They could be especially large for landing and much smaller for cruising at 35,000 feet.)

ORDERING OUT FOR PIZZA

For in-flight emergencies, like running out of soft drinks or pizza, why not include an "errand" plane? The errand plane could fly off to pick up supplies and rejoin your plane later.

Something like that has actually been done. The McDonnell Aircraft Corporation, now called McDonnell Douglas, built the world's smallest jet fighter in 1948 to ride on a bomber. The fighter, the XF-85 Goblin, could be launched and recovered by the bomber. If enemy fighters attacked the bomber, the Goblins would defend it.

GOFER 1

- **What will you call your plane?** You can't have a competitive design without a catchy name. Will you use a number like 757, a letter-number combination like L-1011 (the "L" stands for Lockheed.), or a name like the Airbus? Will you name it after you?

TRY THIS

By Sea and By Air

Many of the words used on board airplanes came from words used at sea. Find the words in this word search that are used on both ships and airplanes. Words run up, down, across, and diagonally in both directions.

Aft

Bulkhead

Captain

Deck

Forward

Galley

Head

Navigation

Pilot

Piloting

Port

Propeller

Rudder

Starboard

N	C	I	B	B	F	D	F	V	D	C	H	C	G	O
A	V	N	U	T	C	B	P	R	M	T	F	A	K	E
V	J	Q	L	D	R	A	A	I	J	G	L	N	K	Q
I	V	R	K	P	R	O	P	E	L	L	E	R	B	Q
G	I	R	H	D	B	A	P	T	E	O	U	W	I	P
A	L	Q	E	R	X	R	W	Y	A	Y	T	W	L	U
T	M	C	A	D	T	T	M	R	T	I	H	I	O	C
I	K	T	D	Y	D	Z	N	K	O	R	N	Q	N	X
O	S	A	P	H	H	U	W	U	L	F	Y	W	R	G
N	E	J	S	V	H	U	R	A	I	A	N	Y	V	D
H	R	R	D	I	R	C	J	V	P	O	H	Y	F	W

See answer page 88.

Do You Want To Sell Your Plane?

Airplanes are expensive. The 1997 sticker price for a Boeing 747-400 is between 156 and 174 million dollars, depending on options.

HOW MUCH PAINT SHOULD YOU ORDER?

Pick any color you want, but you better send someone in a truck to pick it up. It takes 400 pounds of paint to paint a 747.

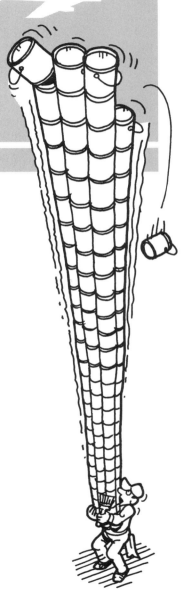

$200,000,000

6 LANDING

The pilot cuts back on the throttle and the plane starts to descend while you are still many miles from your destination. You can hear and feel the change in the sounds and vibrations made by the engines. Soon you will notice the pressure building up in your ears as the plane loses altitude.

As you descend, air pressure in the atmosphere increases, just as water pressure increases the deeper you dive in a pool. The increasing pressure pushes on your eardrums and can become painful. The way to relieve the pressure is to increase pressure on the other side of the eardrums. You do that by swallowing or by exhaling through your nose while pinching it shut.

If there are more planes than the airport can handle at one time, the controllers may have the pilot fly in a **holding pattern**. This is an oval in the sky with planes separated by 1,000 feet. The first plane into the holding pattern goes to the bottom of the stack, and the next plane is stacked 1,000 feet above the first. Controllers keep stacking them up to the limit of their air-

space, maybe 10,000 feet. To stack them higher, controllers have to get clearance from other controllers who manage the upper airspace. If one stack becomes full of planes, the controllers can start to fill another one.

TUNE IN Now is a great time to listen to the pilot and air traffic controllers on your earphones. You can hear controllers direct your pilot to fly at a specific altitude, direction, and speed. As soon as an instruction is given, you can feel the plane move in response. Listen as your pilot identifies your plane by its flight number and the control tower responds by repeating it. Tune in and enjoy the show.

Plane Smart

➤ Birds of a Feather

Birds and airplanes land much the same way. Both extend their wings and flaps to provide more lift at low speed and to add drag to slow them down. Watch the flaps on the airplane wings as your pilot gets ready to land. Next time you watch a bird land, see if it does the same thing.

RECORD FOR STACKING Be glad you weren't on this flight. The all-time record for stacking occurred in 1946 above Washington, D.C. A plane circled for five hours before landing. Do you think they ran out of peanuts and soft drinks? Planes carry extra fuel just in case they get delays like this one.

Pilots want to land going into the wind so they have as much air moving over the wings as possible for maximum lift. Planes need lift to stay up, and the faster they go, the more lift they generate. But when they slow down to land, they need all the lift they can get, and flying into a breeze gives them more lift at slower aircraft speed.

The pilot reduces the speed, extends the flaps to provide more lift, extends the landing gear, and descends. The plane flies about 150 miles per hour in this final approach. Now, even the flight attendants have to sit down. The final approach may seem to take as long as the rest of the flight did, but it only takes about five minutes.

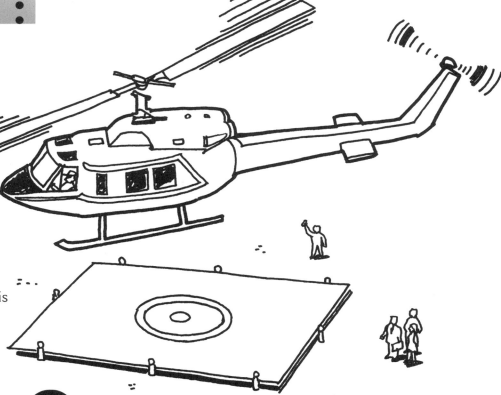

Flying at slow speeds is difficult. You may notice the ride is bumpier. The pilots are working hard now to keep the plane exactly in line for landing.

When pilots need to slow down more, they may raise the **spoilers**, which are flaps on the top of the wings. If they are going too slowly, the pilots will increase the engine thrust. If they do, you will hear the engines roar back to life.

Once the wheels touch down, pilots extend all the flaps and spoilers and reverse the thrust of the engines. Listen for the sharp whine as the engines speed up in reverse.

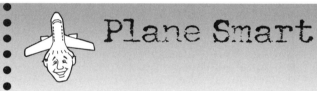

WHOA! In propeller planes, pilots can reverse the thrust of the engines by changing the pitch of the propellers. It would be difficult and time-consuming to stop the engines and start them spinning in the opposite direction to reverse the thrust. Instead the engines continue spinning in the same direction and the propeller blades are rotated around their shafts so they contact air at a different angle.

Plane Smart

> ## Outta Sight

To help the pilots, especially in inclement weather, there is an instrument landing system or ILS. The ILS sends radio signals to pilots to guide them to the correct position and glide angle for landing. Even if the pilots can't see the runway, they can land the plane with the ILS.

Cockpit Tour

Now is your chance. Ask if the pilot will show you the cockpit.

As you peer inside, you will see way too many things. Notice first that the left and right sides are nearly identical. The captain, who sits in the left seat, and the first officer, who sits in the right seat, have the same gauges, switches, and levers.

Separating the two pilots is a panel with controls for the engines. You'll see throttles and indicators of engine speed, temperature and fuel flow.

Both pilots have rudder pedals. They can steer the plane by pressing on these. However, they also have to turn the yoke while they do. While they are turning the rudder with their feet, they operate the ailerons by pushing the yoke in the direction of the turn. In a plane, you steer by pushing the rudder pedals while banking the plane with the ailerons.

The yoke also controls the elevator on the tail. To gain altitude, they pull the yoke backward. To lose altitude, they push it forward.

Ahead of the pilots on what you would call a dashboard is the **automatic pilot**. It can fly the plane without human help.

Ask the pilots to point out these systems and have some other questions ready for them. Many pilots like to talk about flying and may have some great stories to tell. Of course, they are also interested in getting home, so don't keep them there too long.

TOO MANY GAUGES? Take a guess at how many gauges and switches there are on the flight deck. On a 747-400, there are 365. Earlier models of the 747 have 971!

Sometimes planes stop before getting to the dock, and people scramble to be first off. But the plane can lurch forward, spewing people everywhere. As anxious as you are, it's better to wait until the captain rings the bell and turns off the seat belt light before getting up.

If you travel to several different airports, check to see how many different ways bags are brought to travelers. In small airports, the handlers may place bags directly on a shelf for you to pick up. In larger airports, they put bags on conveyor belts or carousels. While waiting for your bags to emerge, see if you can come up with a better system for delivering baggage.

Answers

Answers for page 4.

Airport code	City
DEN	Denver, Colorado
JAX	Jacksonville, Florida
FAI	Fairbanks, Alaska
PDX	Portland, Oregon
TPA	Tampa, Florida
ATL	Atlanta, Georgia
IST	Istanbul, Turkey
RDU	Raleigh-Durham, North Carolina
HNL	Honolulu, Hawaii
LIM	Lima, Peru
TGU	Tegucigalpa Honduras
YTO	Toronto, Ontario
HND	Haneda, Japan
SEA	Seattle, Washington

Airport code	City
OAK	Oakland, California
TYO	Tokyo, Japan
SLC	Salt Lake City
BWI	Baltimore, Maryland
SFO	San Francisco, California
STL	St. Louis, Missouri
MEM	Memphis, Tennessee
ORD	Chicago, Illinois
BZE	Belize City, Belize
ANC	Anchorage, Alaska
DFW	Dallas-Ft. Worth, Texas
GEG	Spokane, Washington
SDA	Baghdad, Iraq
YEA	Edmonton, Alberta

Answers for page 5.

O'Hare	Chicago	Will Rogers	Oklahoma City
Dulles	Washington, D.C.	John Wayne	Orange County, California
Logan	Boston		
Sky Harbor	Phoenix	McCarran	Las Vegas
Midway	Chicago	National	Washington, D.C.
Hartsfield	Atlanta	Hopkins	Cleveland
Kennedy	New York	Mid-continent	Wichita, Kansas
Lindbergh	San Diego	Rickenbacker	Columbus
La Guardia	New York		

Puzzle solution for page 65.

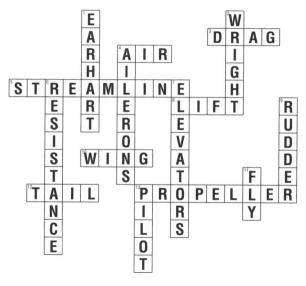

Answers for page 61.

Answers for page iv.

```
T  Y  (B  E  L  L  I)  (C  T  G  D
O  (B  O  E  I  N  G)  U  Z  L  B
W  (J  A  N  N  U  S)  R  E  M  (Y
Q  E  U  P  D  K  J   T  P  A  E
I  (W  I  L  B  U  R)  I  P  A  A
X  S  E  M  E  X  C   S  E  C  G
E  V  X  I  R  L  U   S  L  R  E
(M  O  N  T  G  O  L  F  I  E  R)
I  (E  A  R  H  A  R  T)  N  A  S
S  T  (O  R  V  I  L  L  E)  D  D
M  P  (B  L  E  R  I  O  T)  Y  A
```

Answers for page 79.

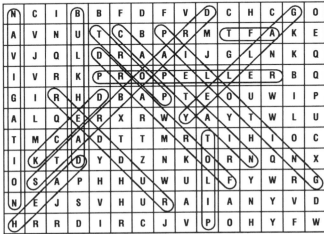

State	Identification	State	Identification
Alabama	Named after an island in England	Missouri	The Lewis and Clark Expedition started here
Alaska	The state bird is the Willow ptarmigan	Montana	This is the fourth largest state in area
Arizona	Has a cactus as the state flower	Nebraska	Part of the Great American Desert
Arkansas	Ozark Mountains are found here	Nevada	Means snow-clad in Spanish
California	State motto is Eureka	New Hampshire	Home of the tallest mountain in New England
Colorado	State name was derived from the Spanish word for red	New Jersey	Named after an island in England
		New Mexico	This state bird prefers running to flying
Connecticut	State name derived from Mohican word for long river place	New York	The only state that has coastlines along the Great Lakes and Atlantic Ocean
Delaware	The first of these United States	North Carolina	Where Orville and Wilbur made history
Florida	This state was name by Ponce de Leon during his search for the Fountain of Youth	North Dakota	Often has the coldest spot in the US in winter
		Ohio	Home to inventors Thomas Edison, the Wright Brothers and Charles Kettering
Georgia	General Sherman marched to the sea through this state	Oklahoma	Nicknamed for people who sneaked in early to claim the best lands
Hawaii	This state was once a kingdom		
Idaho	The Gem State	Oregon	The Beaver State
Illinois	Stephen Douglas debated Abraham Lincoln here	Pennsylvania	The keystone state
		Rhode Island	The Ocean State
Indiana	State name means land of the Indians	South Carolina	Where the Civil War started
Iowa	93% of the land in this state is farms	South Dakota	Home of Mt. Rushmore
Kansas	State song is "Home On The range"	Tennessee	The volunteer state
Kentucky	Home to the most famous horse race	Texas	This state was a separate country briefly
Louisiana	The Pelican State	Utah	Home of Bryce Canyon National Park
Maine	The largest New England state	Vermont	State name is derived from French meaning green mountain
Maryland	The northern border of this state was the Mason-Dixon Line	Virginia	Home of eight U.S. presidents
Massachusetts	Home of the country's most famous tea party	Washington	Only state named for a U.S. president
Michigan	Only state in the continental US that has sections (not islands) entirely separated by water	West Virginia	This state broke away from another state that was trying to break away from the United States
Minnesota	Extends farthest north of the 48 contiguous states	Wisconsin	Home of the cheese heads
Mississippi	The state of Mocking Birds and Magnolias	Wyoming	Lowest population of any state

FLIGHT LOG

Date:_____

Flying from: _____   Flying to: _____

Stops: _____

Flying with _____   Alone _____

Airline(s): _____, _____

Types of Airplanes: _____, _____

Weather Conditions:_____

    Bumpy index: 1.___ (Smooth)

                    2.___ (I felt a bump or two)

                    3.___ (It was okay, really)

                    4.___ (I'm glad it's over)

                    5.___ (Yes, I did use a bag)

Cruising altitude: _____

Average air speed: _____ MPH

Length of flight: _____

Next to me was: _____

The movie was: _____

  Rating: ___ 👍 or ___ 👎

Meals and snacks: ___ 👍 ___ 👎

What I saw out my window: _____

_____

_____

The landing was: ___ (I could have slept through it)

                       ___ (Boring)

                       ___ (Average)

                       ___ (Interesting)

                       ___ (Exciting)

My luggage arrived: ___ (in the same airport as I did, at nearly the same time)

                       ___ (in a different time zone)

                       ___ (we're still waiting)

Who was there to meet us: _____

_____

What we did at our destination: _____

_____

_____

_____

Next destination:_____

_____

_____

FLIGHT LOG

Date:_____

Flying from: _____   Flying to: _____

Stops: _____

Flying with _____   Alone _____

Airline(s): _____, _____

Types of Airplanes: _____, _____

Weather Conditions:_____

    Bumpy index: 1.___ (Smooth)

                     2.___ (I felt a bump or two)

                     3.___ (It was okay, really)

                     4.___ (I'm glad it's over)

                     5.___ (Yes, I did use a bag)

Cruising altitude: _____

Average air speed: _____ MPH

Length of flight: _____

Next to me was: _____

The movie was: _____

   Rating: ___ 👍 or ___ 👎

Meals and snacks: ___ 👍 ___ 👎

What I saw out my window: _____

_____

_____

The landing was: ___ (I could have slept through it)

                          ___ (Boring)

                          ___ (Average)

                          ___ (Interesting)

                          ___ (Exciting)

My luggage arrived: ___ (in the same airport as I did, at nearly the same time)

                          ___ (in a different time zone)

                          ___ (we're still waiting)

Who was there to meet us: _____

_____

What we did at our destination: _____

_____

_____

Next destination:_____

_____

_____

FLIGHT LOG

Date:_____

Flying from: _____   Flying to: _____

Stops: _____

Flying with _____   Alone _____

Airline(s): _____, _____

Types of Airplanes: _____, _____

Weather Conditions:_____

    Bumpy index: 1.___ (Smooth)

                    2.___ (I felt a bump or two)

                    3.___ (It was okay, really)

                    4.___ (I'm glad it's over)

                    5.___ (Yes, I did use a bag)

Cruising altitude: _____

Average air speed: _____ MPH

Length of flight: _____

Next to me was: _____

The movie was: _____

   Rating: ___ 👍 or ___ 👎

Meals and snacks: ___ 👍 ___ 👎

What I saw out my window: _____

_____

_____

The landing was: ___ (I could have slept through it)

                     ___ (Boring)

                     ___ (Average)

                     ___ (Interesting)

                     ___ (Exciting)

My luggage arrived: ___ (in the same airport as I did, at nearly the same time)

                     ___ (in a different time zone)

                     ___ (we're still waiting)

Who was there to meet us: _____

_____

What we did at our destination: _____

_____

_____

Next destination:_____

_____

_____